D1173733

The History of the RAF

FROM 1939 TO THE PRESENT

PA474
PM

The History of the RAF

FROM 1939 TO THE PRESENT

Christopher Chant

CE
CAXTON EDITIONS

This edition published 1999 by
Caxton Edition
An imprint of The Caxton Book Company

Printed 1989, 1990, 1993, 1994, 1996. Fully updated and revised in 1993.

All post-1989 revisions and text by Hugh W. Cowin

ISBN 1 84067 1092

Printed in Indonesia

Main picture: Entering service in 1957, the Vulcan strategic bomber was for almost 30 years the RAF's main nuclear strike carrier. It also set a world record when Vulcan bombers hit Stanley Airport in 1982 during the Falklands War having completed the longest bombing run in history

Title pages: The Lancaster of the Battle of Britain Memorial Flight

Front cover: Armed with two BAe Dynamics ALARM missiles slung beneath its belly, this Tornado GR1 retains its overall Desert Pink colour scheme adopted for the 1991 Gulf War.

REARMING FOR WAR

The Royal Air Force celebrated the silver jubilee of King George V in July 1935 by staging the biggest flypast that had ever been seen. In the morning of 6 July the king visited RAF Mildenhall where a total of 356 aircraft and their crews, representing 25 regular and 12 auxiliary squadrons as well as coast defence units, formed a static display. In the afternoon he was driven to RAF Duxford, where he watched as 20 of the squadrons from Mildenhall flew overhead.

However, the aircraft themselves were ominously old-fashioned. Two squadrons of Heyfords, five of Harts, two of Audaxes, one of Demons, six of Bulldogs and three of Furys, representing the heavy and light bomber, army co-operation and fighter strength of the force, were followed by No 19 Squadron with the newest fighter, the Gloster Gauntlet. The Heyfords maintained the stately pace of 98 mph (158 km/h), while the fighters were hardly more exciting at 120 mph (193 km/h).

The Gauntlet had entered service with No 19 Squadron only two months before the flypast, yet it was derived from the Gloster SS.18 which had flown for the first time as long ago as January 1929. The SS.18 had actually been a contender for the fighter contract that went instead to the Bristol Bulldog, but now the Gauntlet was in production as a Bulldog replacement, and within two years 14 squadrons would be equipped with the type: expansion was under way, but for the time being it would be based on clearly obsolescent aircraft.

At the beginning of 1935 the first examples of the Vickers Vincent, a general purpose derivative of the Vildebeest, had entered service as a replacement for the Fairey IIIFs and Westland Wapitis with the overseas squadrons. Slightly better performance was offered by another new general purpose type, the Hawker Hardy version of the Hart bomber. The first of the 47 built went to No 30 Squadron in Iraq in April, and were later passed on to two other squadrons in the Middle East and East Africa. In September and November the two bomber transport squadrons in the Middle East received Valentias, essentially Victoria Mk VIs under another name, and most of which were simply Victorias fitted with slightly more powerful models of the Pegasus engine.

The only new aircraft to show any real innovation was the Boulton Paul Overstrand, a stronger, more powerful and more comfortable development of the company's earlier Sidestrand. The main interest in the Overstrand, however, was its pneumatically operated nose turret, which balanced the weight of the gunner on his seat against the weight of the installation to give automatic traverse and elevation as the gunner

Previous page: An early production Hawker Hurricane Mk I

Bristol Bulldogs of No 17 Squadron. The Bulldog was still one of the principal RAF fighters in 1935

adjusted his aim. No 101 Squadron was the only unit to operate the Overstrand, which was still fitted with a fixed undercarriage, and the single Lewis gun mounted in the turret seemed hardly worth such an elaborate mounting.

Nevertheless, in the absence of anything better, it was decided that new squadrons should continue to be formed with light bombers, so that at least there would be trained crews for the new, advanced types that were currently being ordered off the drawing board in an attempt to cut out the lengthy development process.

Accordingly, the next new type to appear was the Hawker Hind, which began to enter service in the following January. Yet another Hart derivative, the Hind embodied few major changes apart from the use of a fully supercharged Kestrel V engine and a cut-down rear cockpit to improve the gunner's field of fire. The new model superseded the Hart in six home-based day bomber squadrons, but more important were the 25 new squadrons that were formed with Hinds between 1936 and 1938, while altogether 14 auxiliary squadrons used the type. By 1939 all the new squadrons had converted to new monoplane bombers.

In the meantime, expansion scheme A had been superseded by the much more ambitious scheme F, approved by the Cabinet in February 1936. The increased urgency that had provoked this and a series of earlier new schemes derived from the realisation in the spring of 1935 that the new German air force, the Luftwaffe, was already bigger than the RAF. The overall aim of scheme F was an air force of 161 squadrons, 124 of them based in Britain, by March 1939. The home force was to consist of 68 squadrons of bombers, 30 of fighters, two of torpedo bombers, seven land-based and six flying-boat reconnaissance squadrons and 11 for army co-operation.

The new scheme restored the emphasis on bombers, which was Trenchard's legacy. Not the least of its requirements was an increase in the total number of home-based aircraft from 547 to 1736. Overseas strength was to enjoy a less dramatic but still substantial increase from 24 to 37 squadrons, representing 468 aircraft instead of the 265 in March 1934. Moreover, the single-engined day bombers were to be replaced by the new medium bombers, which would equip a total of 48 squadrons, and adequate war reserves were to be provided by raising the initial establishment of 29 of them from 12 aircraft to 18. The underlying intention was to build an air force strong enough to deter any German attack through the Low Countries and Belgium.

As it happened, while this new scheme was being worked out a major overseas deployment was under way. Following the Italian invasion of Ethiopia in October 1935 several squadrons were shipped to the Middle East while some of those already in the area were moved nearer to the war zone, though there was no direct intervention in the conflict. A squadron of IIIFs moved from Egypt to the Sudan, where it was joined by two squadrons of Gordons from Britain, and another squadron of Gordons was formed in Kenya. A squadron each of Demons and Harts were shipped to Aden, two similar units going as reinforcements to Egypt, where a third Demon squadron was formed, and a squadron of Vildebeest torpedo bombers and another new Demon squadron were based on Malta. Flying boats were also deployed, with the Singapore squadron from Iraq moving to Aden, Rangoons and Stranraers – the latter being improved Southamptons – stationed in Gibraltar, and a squadron of Supermarine Scapas, also derived from the Southampton, with another of Singapores based in Egypt. All these remained at their new bases until October 1936, some months after the Italian invasion had been completed.

By this time the first really modern aircraft were in service, in the form of the Avro Anson. This was based on a commercial airliner, and became the RAF's first monoplane with a retractable undercarriage when the first examples joined No 48 Squadron for air-crew training in March 1936. Both the undercarriage and the dorsal turret were manually operated, but the Anson gave excellent service as a trainer – during 1936 No 48 had no less than 80 on strength at the School of Air Navigation at Manston – as well as serving with coastal reconnaissance squadrons.

Three months later the old ADGB Command was replaced by four new commands. Bomber, Fighter, Coastal and Training Commands, each with its own headquarters, were constituted with respective strengths of six, three, three and four groups. At the same time, in order to meet the demand for new aircraft and engines the government financed a system of 'shadow' factories which were operated by various motor car manufacturers. Initially, five companies were involved in the production of the Bristol Pegasus and Mercury engines that were in greatest demand, some in the production of components which the others assembled.

Among the first to benefit from the new supply of engines was the Handley Page Harrow, which was also one of the first of the new bombers ordered at the design stage without waiting for a prototype. Five squadrons were equipped with Harrows during 1937, and the type was notable for its use of powered turrets in both nose and tail positions. These turrets still

AKX 386

Previous page: King George V and party with Rolls-Royces in front of a Handley Page Heyford at RAF Mildenhall, Suffolk, during the Jubilee Review, 6 July 1935

The Bristol Blenheim I was one of the most advanced types in service when it joined No 114 Squadron in March 1937

mounted only a single Lewis gun, but they embodied a driving mechanism produced by Nash and Thompson, whose turrets were to become standard equipment on the RAF's heavy bombers.

The Harrow was also a monoplane, though not the first monoplane heavy bomber: the previous November No 38 Squadron had received the Fairey Hendon, six years after the prototype had flown for the first time. Only 14 Hendons were built, and No 38 was the only squadron to be fully equipped with the type, though one flight was detached to reform No 115 Squadron in June 1937.

November 1936 also saw the appearance in service of the Fury II, with a more powerful 640-hp Kestrel VI engine and fairings on the undercarriage wheels. The Fury II was produced as a replacement for the Fury Is while a more extensively revised version using the ultimately unsuccessful steam-cooled Goshawk engine was under development. The latter had been developed to meet a 1930 specification for a new fighter having a top speed of at least 250 mph (403 km/h), carrying four Vickers guns and with improved performance all round. The further specification of the Goshawk engine meant that none of the aircraft originally designed to meet this requirement was acceptable, and in the end the Mercury-engined Gloster Gladiator, a development of the Gauntlet, was ordered instead.

The first Gladiators joined a flight of No 1 Squadron to form No 72 Squadron in February 1937, and the RAF's last biplane fighter was significant in its doubling of the previously accepted armament of two Vickers machine guns. Two of these were in the nose and one in each lower wing, and the Vickers guns were subsequently replaced by .303-in Brownings, with the considerably higher rate of fire of 1200 rds/min. The Gladiator had an enclosed cockpit, but was otherwise outmoded for a fighter of the late 1930s, having a fixed-pitch wooden airscrew and offering no armour protection for the pilot. Nevertheless, eight fighter squadrons were equipped with Gladiators during

1937, and while these were soon superseded by Hurricanes and Spitfires, the type saw service subsequently in the Middle East, usually only briefly as equipment for newly formed squadrons.

The spring of 1937 also saw the arrival of several of the new bombers produced under the expansion scheme, with Whitleys, Blenheims, Battles and Wellesleys all entering service in March and April. The Armstrong Whitworth Whitley had been designed to meet the same specification as the Harrow, and was at first armed with single Vickers guns in manually operated nose and tail turrets. However, the Mk III version introduced a powered turret for the nose guns, with an additional retractable ventral turret mounting two Brownings, and the Mk IV dispensed with the ventral installation in favour of a four-gun Nash and Thompson tail turret. The main production version, the Mk V of 1939, extended the tail slightly to give the rear gunner a better field of fire.

The Bristol Blenheim, by contrast, was armed with the traditional single forward-firing Vickers, though this was mounted in the port wing and was soon replaced by a Browning, and a Lewis gun for rearward defence. A retractable turret had replaced the old Scarff ring as a mounting, and the gun itself was replaced by the Vickers gas-operated, as opposed to recoil-operated, K gun. The Blenheim's main form of defence was, however, its speed, which at 285 mph (459 km/h) allowed it to outpace most contemporary fighters with ease. This, in turn, was a result of its truly modern design, incorporating such features as stressed skin construction, retractable undercarriage and variable-pitch propellers. On the other hand, only 1000 lb (454 kg) of bombs could be carried, and the type was to remain in production long after it had become obsolescent.

The other two new bombers were both single-engined, the last such aircraft to be built for the RAF. The Fairey Battle was produced to meet a 1932 specification for a day bomber able to carry 1000 lb (454 kg) of bombs 1000 miles (1609 km) at 200 mph (322 km/h). Although these figures represented considerable improvements over those of the Harts and Hinds the new bomber was intended to replace, neither the Battle's maximum speed of 241 mph (388 km/h) nor its armament of single wing-mounted Browning and manually aimed Vickers K gun would offer much protection against the new fighters it was to meet in combat a few years later.

The Vickers Wellesley was the first RAF aircraft to use the geodetic form of construction originally developed by Barnes Wallis for the airship *R.100*. Composed of small sections of rolled or pressed light alloy riveted together in basket-work fashion, the geodetic method had the dual advantages of reduced weight and ease of repair, though it precluded an internal bomb bay and the Wellesley's bombs were carried in nacelles under the wings. As well as serving

with six Bomber Command squadrons, the Wellesley was used by the Long-Range Development Flight to establish a new distance record of 7162 miles (11,526 km) in November 1938, when two examples completed a flight from Ismailia in Egypt to Darwin in northern Australia.

An indication of the sort of opposition the new bombers would have to face came towards the end of 1937 with the introduction of the Hawker Hurricane. The RAF's first fighter capable of exceeding 300 mph (483 km/h) in level flight under operational conditions, the Hurricane mounted four Brownings in each wing and was powered by a Rolls-Royce Merlin engine. And with its rate of climb of better than 2000 ft/min (610 m/min) the Hurricane at last offered the possibility of mounting an effective defence against attacks by the new generation of high-speed bombers.

This was an important development. In 1934 it had been concluded by a committee set up to investigate the problem that the increasing speed of bombers was presenting the fighters designed to intercept them with an almost impossible problem: enemy bombers crossing the coast of Britain at a height of 10,000 ft (3048 m) or more and a speed of over 200 mph (322 km/h) would have reached their targets in London or the Midlands before the fighters could get within range. In the absence of a warning system to provide advance notice of the bombers' approach, the only way to intercept them would be to maintain standing patrols of fighters, and given the length of coastline it would be necessary to patrol, this was bound to be an impossibly costly system to maintain. Coupled with the government's policy of achieving parity with the Luftwaffe – initially taken to mean simple equality of numbers, and later amended to indicate an equivalent striking power – the emphasis continued to be on the provision of more bombers at the expense of fighters.

However, in December 1937 a different strategy began to take shape. The Air Staff had been asked to provide estimates for the strength necessary to counter the threat from Germany, and their response was a predictable recommendation for more squadrons of bigger bombers. This was rejected by Sir Thomas Inskip, who in March 1936 had been appointed Minister for the Co-ordination of Defence: instead, Inskip suggested that the best defence against German bombing attacks would be defensive fighters rather than bombers. His reasoning was that Germany was not in a position to fight a long war any more than Britain was in a position to win a short one, and that it might be sounder policy to take advantage of Germany's weakness. With the new fighters now in production, and, equally importantly, with the aid of the early warning provided by the new radar equipment,

it would at last be possible to mount an effective defence against bomber attacks.

Accordingly, it was decided to concentrate on building up fighter reserves, and during 1938 the Hurricane was joined in production by a second new fighter, the Supermarine Spitfire. Also based on the Merlin engine and armed with eight wing-mounted Brownings, the Spitfire was of considerably more modern design than the Hurricane, using stressed-skin construction. Whereas the Hurricane carried its guns close to the fuselage with the undercarriage retracting inwards, the Spitfire reversed the process, with a narrow-track undercarriage retracting outwards towards the wingtips and the guns carried further outboard in the distinctive broad-chord elliptical wings. In combination, the two types formed an excellent partnership: the Hurricane was more straightforward to build, so that large numbers could be provided relatively quickly, while the Spitfire, requiring considerably more work in the manufacturing process, offered correspondingly higher performance and an astonishing capacity for improvement.

The second vital component of the air defence system, the radio detection equipment (radar), was also in an advanced stage of development by 1938. The first exercise to test the technique of ground controlled interception (GCI) during 1936 had produced such promising results that work was started on building a string of radar stations known as Chain Home, which were later supplemented by Chain Home Low stations to guard against the approach of low-flying aircraft. By the beginning of 1938 fighters from Biggin Hill in Kent were being directed by the original station at Bawdsey, in Suffolk, to intercept airliners approaching Croydon airport from the continent.

At the same time, a system of operational control was being developed. From the individual stations, reports were transmitted to Bentley Priory, near Stanmore in Middlesex, where Air Chief Marshal Sir Hugh Dowding, Commander-in-Chief of Fighter Command, had his headquarters. Here the reports from the various stations were compared and evaluated in the Filter Room, before the positions of attacking and defending aircraft were plotted on a map table for transmission to the various operations rooms that were established at the headquarters of each Fighter Group as well as at Fighter Command HQ. In September 1938 there were two groups, No 11 with 19 squadrons and No 12 with 12, the former concentrated south of Bedford and the latter extending north of Bedford as far as York.

Another component of Fighter Command was No 30 Balloon Group, whose 10 squadrons in London,

A Canadian-built Hurricane IIB preserved by the Strathallan Collection

Right: Vickers Wellesleys of the Long-Range Development Flight, which established a new world distance record of 7162 miles (11,526 km) in November 1938

Far right: The Armstrong Whitworth Whitley was another of the RAF's new monoplane bombers, entering service in 1937

Surrey, Middlesex and Essex were deployed during the Munich crisis in September 1938. A few weeks later, on 1 November, No 30 became Balloon Command, and during the next year a further three groups were formed. No 31 included seven squadrons based around Birmingham, five around Manchester, three around Liverpool and one in the Derby area. No 32 included three squadrons defending Bristol, two each for Portsmouth and Southampton and one for Cardiff; and No 33 included the three squadrons each allocated to Newcastle-upon-Tyne, Hull, Sheffield and Glasgow. The number of balloons each squadron operated varied from 16 to 45; they were deployed from light trucks or, in coastal areas, barges, and their job was to create barriers of steel cables suspended from the balloons to force attacking aircraft to fly higher than the 5000 ft (1524 m) or so to which the balloons were set, thus bringing them within range of the anti-aircraft guns and discouraging low-level attacks.

Earlier that year, too, the rapid build-up of equipment for the growing number of squadrons was reflected in the formation of Maintenance Command. This organisation took over responsibility for all supply depots. The potential for aircraft production was expanded by the establishment of facilities in Canada, as well as by orders placed with manufacturers in the United States, both of which would become important sources of new aircraft.

Meanwhile, the new emphasis on defence did not mean that the supply of new types of bomber had ceased. A 1932 specification for a twin-engined day bomber to carry a 1000-lb (454-kg) bombload over a range of 720 miles (1159 km) and with a maximum range of 1500 miles (2414 km) resulted in two new types, first of which was the Handley Page Hampden. The Hampden entered service in September 1938 and proved capable of delivering a 4000-lb (1814-kg) load of bombs, but despite its makers' claims for it as a 'fighter bomber', and the provision of a fixed forward-firing machine gun, the defensive armament of single hand-held machine guns in nose, dorsal and ventral positions proved completely inadequate.

The second bomber resulting from the same specification joined No 9 Squadron the following February. This was the Vickers Wellington, which, like the Wellesley, was constructed using the geodetic system. Unlike the Wellesley, however, it had an internal bomb bay big enough for nine 500-lb (227-kg) bombs, which it could carry for 2000 miles (3219 km), and with a similar number of 250-lb (113-kg) bombs the range was extended to 3000 miles (4828 km). Armament comprised twin Brownings in powered nose and tail turrets, and early examples also had a retractable ventral turret, though this was soon abandoned.

The Wellington was the last new bomber to join Bomber Command before the outbreak of war in September 1939, by which time it was in service with all eight squadrons of No 3 Group as well as two squadrons of No 6 Group. The remainder of No 6 comprised five squadrons of Battles, three of Blenheims and

Right: Vickers Wellingtons of No 30 Operational Training Unit

KD
BT T
BT Z
BK347

two each of Hampdens and Whitleys. While No 3 was an operational group, with two of its squadrons being reserve units, No 6 was engaged in operational training.

No 1 Group Bomber Command at this time consisted of 10 squadrons of Battles, and following the order for mobilisation of all RAF units on 23 August No 1 was reconstituted as the Advanced Air Striking Force. The AASF was in turn divided into five wings, Nos 71, 72, 74, 75 and 76, of two squadrons each, and on 2 September, in accordance with existing plans, these flew to French bases in the Rheims area, a matter of hours before England and France declared war on Germany.

No 2 Group was equipped with Blenheims, with six operational and one reserve squadron divided into Nos 82, 83 and 79 Wings. No 4 Group's six squadrons of Whitleys included one reserve squadron, and No 5's eight squadrons of Whitleys included two reserve squadrons. Thus Bomber Command's home-based operational strength amounted to six squadrons each of Blenheims, Wellingtons and Whitleys and Hampdens, and five of Whitleys.

Fighter Command, in the year since the Munich agreement, had reached a position of much greater strength. All the Furys and Demons, and the bulk of the Gauntlets, had been replaced by Hurricanes, Spitfires and Blenheims, though there were still four squadrons of Gladiators. The formation or mobilisation of an additional eight squadrons had enabled a new group, No 10, to be formed for the protection of the southwest of the country.

Coastal Command was rather less well equipped. Its three groups, No 18 based in Scotland, No 16 in southeastern England and No 15 covering western England and the Irish Sea, disposed of a total of 19 squadrons, including six of flying boats. The land-based reconnaissance squadrons included 10 of Ansons and two of Vildebeests, both of which were obsolescent by this stage, and only one squadron was equipped with the new Lockheed Hudson that had been ordered in 1938 by the first purchasing mission to the United

Below: A Vickers Wellington X after post-war conversion for training duties

An Avro Manchester prepares for take-off, with a Vickers Wellington in the distance

States. Based on the Lockheed Super Electra, an 11-seat passenger aircraft, the Hudson was powered by a pair of 1100-hp Wright Cyclone radial engines and armed with twin Brownings in a powered dorsal turret.

Coastal Command's flying boat squadrons were hardly better off. One squadron was still flying Stranraers, and another three were equipped with Saunders-Roe Londons, the latter being twin-engined biplanes that were clearly obsolescent. One of the London squadrons, however, was in the process of converting to Sunderlands, which also formed the equipment of the remaining two flying-boat squadrons.

The Short Sunderland was developed from the Short C Class Empire passenger flying boat in the mid-1930s, and was a four-engined all-metal monoplane. It was armed with powered turrets in the bow and stern, the former with a single Browning and the latter with four, plus single manually aimed Vickers K guns on each side of the beam, while up to 2000 lb (907 kg) of bombs, depth charges or mines could be carried. With its long range and roomy interior the Sunderland was to prove highly adaptable, serving principally as a convoy escort and maritime patrol aircraft, but also proving useful for air-sea rescue and emergency transport and claiming an impressive number of victims in aerial combat.

The army co-operation squadrons were in an equally poor state. In addition to two squadrons of Blenheims and four of Hurricanes which had been allocated to form part of the Air Component, British Expeditionary Force, there were five operational and two reserve squadrons in existence in August 1939. One of the reserve squadrons was still using Hawker Hinds, and the other Hawker Hectors, another Hart derivative produced as an interim replacement for the Audax.

The remaining five army co-operation squadrons were by now standardised on the Westland Lysander, a two-seat high-wing monoplane with fixed undercarriage that had been designed to meet a specification issued in 1935. The undercarriage fairings each accommodated a Browning machine gun, whose ammunition was fed through the fairings from boxes in the fuselage, and stub wings could be fitted to allow up to 500 lb (227 kg) of bombs to be carried. The observer in the rear of the enclosed cockpit had the time-honoured single Lewis gun, though this was later replaced by twin Brownings, and the outstanding quality of the Lysander was its very low minimum flying speed of 59 mph (95 km/h). Its top speed was 229 mph (368 km/h), and the makers' optimistic suggestion that the Lysander's low-flying qualities might enable it to out-manoeuvre faster enemy fighters was unfortunately not borne out by experience.

While the deteriorating situation in Europe had focussed attention on home defence and the build-up of the bomber force at home, the RAF still had considerable overseas commitments. Egypt remained the centre of activities in the Middle East, and the RAF Command there included five squadrons of Blenheims, three of Gladiators, two of Valentia bomber transports and one each of Lysanders and Wellesleys. In addition, the Sudan Wing comprised a squadron of Wellesleys based at Nairobi and another of mixed Wellesleys and Vincents at Khartoum. A single squadron based at Ramleh came under the Palestine and Transjordan Command, and this included Hardys, Gauntlets and Lysanders on its strength. British Forces in Iraq had been reduced to a single squadron of Blenheims at Shaibah, while the Aden Command comprised one squadron of Vincents and Blenheims, a second of Gladiators and a third of Singapore flying boats. Another squadron of London flying boats was based on Malta, but immediately after the outbreak of war this was moved to Gibraltar.

Trenchard's plan for the RAF to take over military

control in India had never been put into effect, so the six squadrons there were equipped mainly for army co-operation work. Apart from one squadron of Blenheims and another equipped with Harts and Tiger Moths for training purposes, there were two squadrons of Audaxes and one of Wapitis, plus a bomber transport squadron with Valentias.

Singapore, on the other hand, was regarded as essentially a naval base, since an overland attack through the jungles of Malaya was considered impossible, and the main defences were composed of artillery batteries. These were supplemented by two squadrons of Vildebeest torpedo bombers and two of reconnaissance flying boats, which in August 1939 were equipped with Singapores and Sunderlands. During that month, two squadrons of Blenheims arrived from India to reinforce the colony, and another two Blenheim squadrons were despatched from Britain, arriving during September. Another squadron of Vildebeests based in Ceylon (Sri Lanka) completed RAF Far East Command.

Following the signing of the non-aggression treaty between Germany and the Soviet Union on 23 August 1939, the RAF reserves were mobilised and the force put on a war footing. Two days later the Anglo-Polish treaty of mutual assistance was signed and on 1 September Germany invaded Poland. On 3 September, acting on instructions from London, the British ambassador in Germany delivered an ultimatum calling on Germany to cease hostilities against Poland by 11.00 am. The deadline passed without response from Hitler, and Britain, followed by France, declared war on Germany. The RAF was 21 years old, and for the second time it was involved in a world war. For most of the preceding 20 years of peace it had been on active service somewhere in the world, but now it would be called on to fight over land and sea around the globe.

Wartime scene at a flying boat base, with a Short Sunderland III on the slipway

W4004

THE DEFENSIVE WAR

Within minutes of the prime minister's announcement that Britain was at war with Germany, the air raid sirens sounded over London: an unidentified aircraft had been plotted approaching from the continent. It was soon established that this was nothing more than a French aircraft carrying the assistant air attaché, but three days later there was a more serious alarm.

This time the report came from a searchlight crew in the Thames estuary, and as fighters scrambled to meet the threat they appeared on the radar screens as a growing force of aircraft out to sea. The result was more fighters being ordered into the air, which only added to the confusion, and it was some time before the mistake was realised.

The state of edgy alertness which characterised these incidents was a result of the growing fear of air attack over the previous decade. Almost everyone, whether taking Trenchard's view that the only effective response was the capacity for retaliatory raids, or accepting the idea that fighter defences were the essential requirement, believed that Germany would attempt to knock out Britain by an immediate, all-out aerial bombardment. To that extent, while the false alarms were disturbing, there was some reassurance to be gained from the swiftness of the response.

However, as the weeks passed, it became clear that there was to be no immediate assault on Britain. At the same time, the British bombers were inhibited by political considerations from beginning any full-scale offensive of their own: the French were reluctant to allow such provocative action from continental bases, and the limited range of the bombers available would not allow them to reach targets in Germany without violating Dutch and Belgian neutrality. As it happened, Germany was not in any position to mount a full-scale bombing offensive in any case, since the Luftwaffe had been built up as a tactical air force to support army operations.

Consequently, most of the early air engagements took place at sea, as reconnaissance aircraft encountered each other, anti-shipping strikes were intercepted, and Bomber Command's activities were limited to the dropping of propaganda leaflets and sporadic attacks on German warships. The most immediate problem remained the air force in France.

The RAF was committed to supporting the British Expeditionary Force's 10 divisions in France, and following the arrival of the Advanced Air Striking Force on the day before the declaration of war, four squadrons of Hurricanes and two of Blenheims arrived within the next few days. Four army co-operation squadrons of Lysanders and another two of Blenheims had arrived by the end of October, and in December another two Blenheim squadrons joined them. In that month all the RAF units were incorporated in a new command, British Air Forces in France, under the operational control of the BEF. There were continuing demands for more fighter squadrons, though these were strenuously resisted by Dowding at Fighter Command, whose efforts were concentrated on building up adequate air defences, and who refused to allow any Spitfire squadrons to be based across the Channel.

With the exception of a fifth squadron of Lysanders which joined the BAFF in April 1940, the units that had arrived by the end of December constituted the total RAF force in France until the German invasion began in May. Again, they were limited in their operations both by the French desire to avoid provocation and by the lack of existing facilities, and reconnaissance continued to be their main task until the German Blitzkrieg was launched.

Meanwhile, in April 1940 the German forces occupied Denmark and launched an invasion of Norway in order to pre-empt British plans to mine Norwegian waters and hinder the supply of Swedish iron ore to Germany. Two squadrons of fighters, No 263 with Gladiators and No 46 with Hurricanes, were sent to Norway and these provided some measure of fighter cover. Many of the Gladiators were destroyed on the frozen lake from which they were operating by German bomber attacks, and the surviving fighters were lost following evacuation, when the carrier HMS *Glorious* on which they had embarked was sunk.

By this time the invasion of France was almost over. A further four Hurricane squadrons had been sent to France almost as soon as the fighting began, but the position was hopeless from the start. The Battles and Blenheims were no match for the German fighters – in one raid alone, on 14 May, more than half of a force of 67 Blenheims and Battles were lost in attacks on

Far left: The crew of a Bristol Blenheim I emerge from their aircraft after a flight

Left: Servicing a Westland Lysander in the snow on a French airfield

Previous spread: A Supermarine Spitfire Mk II taxies out as a Fairey Swordfish prepares to land

Above: Fairey Battles prepare to take off from a snow-covered airfield

One of the enduring symbols of the Battle of Britain: the elliptical wings of a Spitfire in flight

bridges and other targets in the area around Sedan – and within a matter of days the army co-operation squadrons were being withdrawn, leaving the bulk of their aircraft behind, either victims of the fighting or destroyed for lack of fuel or equipment.

The AASF squadrons, meanwhile, had been by-passed by the main German advance, and it proved almost impossible to redeploy them. The fighters were in constant action, claiming many victories, but there was inevitable attrition. Altogether, a total of 959 RAF aircraft were lost during May and June, including 432 fighters. Most of the latter were Hurricanes, though there had also been losses among the Spitfire squadrons covering the evacuation of the BEF from Dunkirk, flying at the limit of their range from bases in southeast England. At the same time a high proportion of the 1284 Luftwaffe aircraft lost had been victims of the British fighters.

The evacuation from Dunkirk was completed on 4 June, and on 18 June the last squadrons in France were withdrawn to England. The Luftwaffe was now able to operate from captured bases in northern France, and with the severe depletion of the fighter squadrons that had taken place, the German bombers now constituted a much more serious threat to Britain. Almost half of the total of operational fighters had been lost during May and June, and only record production by the aircraft factories during the months of June and July, when a total of 942 new Spitfires and Hurricanes were delivered, enabled Fighter Command to prepare for the battle that would now take place in the skies over southern England.

In the meantime, German air attacks were concentrated on shipping in the Channel, as preparations for the seaborne invasion of Britain were put in hand. Fighter Command, meanwhile, was being strengthened and reorganised, and by the end of the first week in August it consisted of four groups and a total of 56 squadrons. Among these, however, were six squadrons of the improvised and largely ineffective Blenheim IFs, another squadron which consisted of a single flight of Gladiators, and two more equipped with the Boulton Paul Defiant.

The Defiant was the successor to the two-seater Demon fighters. Produced in response to a 1935 specification, it was armed with four Browning machine guns carried in a powered turret and intended to fly standing patrols, using its guns to attack bombers from below. The first squadron deliveries were not made until December 1939, however, by which time the whole concept had become outmoded: lack of familiarity on the part of German pilots enabled some early successes to be achieved, but as soon as the type's lack of forward-firing guns was appreciated it became easy prey as a day interceptor, and was switched to night fighting.

By August, there were no Defiants left in No 11 Group, whose 13 squadrons of Hurricanes, six of Spitfires and two of Blenheims were based at 13 airfields in the southeast of the country. No 10 Group,

BRITISH AIRFIELDS, 1940
Castletown
Wick
Dyce
Montrose
Leuchars
Grangemouth
Turnhouse
Prestwick
Aldergrove
Acklington
Usworth
Thornaby
Catterick
Dishforth
Linton-on-Ouse
Driffield
Church Fenton
North Coates
Manchester
Kirton-in-Lindsey
Doncaster
Finningley
Hemswell
Scampton
Waddington
Digby
Hucknall
Cottesmore
Bircham Newton
West Raynham
Marham
Watton
Coltishall
Wittering
Upwood
Feltwell
Upper Heyford
Bicester
Mildenhall
Honington
Newmarket
Alconbury
Stradishall
Martlesham
Bassingbourn
Pembrey
Benson
Bibury
Duxford
Castle Camps
Harwell
Debden
North Weald
Stapleford Abbots
Northolt
Hornchurch
Rochford
Croydon
Gravesend
Kenley
Middle Wallop
Biggin Hill
Detling
Manston
Boscombe Down
Hawkinge
Tangmere
St Eval
Exeter
Warmwell
Goodwood
Thorney Island
Plymouth
Fighter Command Airfields
Bomber Command Airfields
Coastal Command Airfields

Pilots of No 111 Squadron race to their Hawker Hurricanes during the battle for France, May 1940

whose territory was southwestern England and South Wales, comprised four squadrons of Spitfires, three of Hurricanes, and single squadrons of Gladiators and Blenheims, the Gladiator unit being only one flight. No 12 Group, with responsibility for the defence of the Midlands, disposed of six squadrons of Spitfires, five of Hurricanes, two of Blenheims and one of Defiants, while to the north of the Humber and the Mersey No 13 Group consisted of nine Hurricane, two Spitfire, one Defiant and one Blenheim squadrons.

With such limited resources, the key to success would be their efficient employment, and in this respect the system that had been built up in the five years of Fighter Command's existence was to prove decisive. Warning of the approach of German bomber formations was provided by the coastal radar stations, and after they had crossed the coast they were tracked by the network of Observer Corps posts. Reports from these were analysed and co-ordinated in the Filter Room at Bentley Priory. The resulting situation reports were duplicated on the Operations Room plotting tables at Fighter Command and Group headquarters, and from the Group the information was passed to the appropriate Sector Operations Room. Each sector was a division of the group, and it was at the sector headquarters that operational control of the squadrons within the sector, and of units in the air, was exercised. After receiving the order to take-off, the pilots were guided to their targets by the sector controllers.

In their efforts, the Fighter Command pilots were assisted by tactical and operational miscalculations on the part of the Luftwaffe. The German bombers were armed with hand-aimed machine guns which proved inevitably inadequate for defence, so that the German fighters were restricted to providing close escorts for the bombers. Thus the Bf 109 pilots, whose machines were in many respects superior to the opposing Hurricanes and Spitfires, were often left to watch in relative helplessness as RAF fighters dived past them to attack the bombers. The Bf 109s, too, were fighting at the limit of their range, while the long-range Bf 110s proved ineffective fighters.

As far as the Luftwaffe was concerned, the Battle of Britain, intended to be the preliminary to the cross-channel invasion, fell into four distinct phases. Following the attacks on Allied shipping in the Channel, which by 25 July succeeded in discouraging any further attempts to send convoys through the Straits of Dover in daylight, there was an attempt to lure the British fighters into the air and destroy them. On 8 August the effort was switched to a bombing offensive against the fighter bases themselves, with supplementary raids on aircraft factories. By the end of the first week of September Fighter Command losses were rapidly outstripping the rate of replacements, but at this point the German offensive was turned against London, and for three weeks daylight raids on the capital were mounted.

The change of emphasis was, to a large extent, the salvation of Fighter Command. Free to operate without the interference of continual attacks on their bases, the Hurricanes and Spitfires were able to blunt the attacks on London, claiming large numbers of bombers destroyed and, in the end, forcing the Luftwaffe to turn to night attacks. More important, the plan to invade Britain, which in turn depended on the destruction of the RAF's fighters, had to be postponed indefinitely.

Combatting the night raids called for new tactics and, before it could be done effectively, new aircraft and new equipment. The Blenheims that had been hopefully fitted out for the task were too slow and too lightly armed to carry out effective interceptions. However, they played an important part in the development of the airborne interception radar that was the main requirement, mainly because they had room to accommodate the bulky equipment and its operator. The first AI radar-equipped Blenheims had begun trials shortly before the outbreak of war, and by April 1940 all six of Fighter Command's Blenheim squadrons were using the new device.

The first success using AI radar was achieved on the night of 22/23 July 1940, but subsequent victories were rare until the Blenheims were replaced by Bristol Beaufighters during the second half of 1940. The Beaufighter was big and heavy, but with two 1560-hp Bristol Hercules engines it was capable of 320 mph (515 km/h), and it carried a heavy armament of four 20-mm Hispano cannon in the nose plus six Brownings in the wings. No radar was fitted until November, by which time five of the six Blenheim squadrons had made the conversion to the new type, but the Mk IV that was then fitted in place of the Mk III equipment used on the Blenheim night fighters was considerably more effective. The first kill came on 11 November, but it was not until January 1941, when GCI equipment that could track both interceptor and quarry became operational, that a useful rate of success began to be achieved.

Three victories for the Beaufighters in that first month were followed by a steadily mounting toll, with 22 kills in March eclipsed by a total of 48 in April and no fewer than 96 in the first 10 days of May. The efforts of the Beaufighters were supplemented by Blenheims carrying out night intruder missions against the bombers' bases, waiting for them to return from the raids and attacking them as they neared home. The last of the major night raids on London was made on the night of 10/11 May 1941, following which the bulk of the Luftwaffe was withdrawn from the bombing offensive against England, to concentrate on the build-up for the German invasion of the Soviet Union.

May 1941 also saw the flight of the first night-fighter version of one of the outstanding aircraft of the war, the De Havilland Mosquito. The Mosquito brought a new level of performance to the job, being capable of almost 50 mph (80 km/h) more than the

De Havilland Mosquito NF.2 night fighters, showing the nose aerials for the airborne interception radar

Beaufighter. The further addition of the AI Mk VIII radar, operating at much shorter wavelengths and able to scan the sky ahead, made the NF.XII version of the Mosquito, which joined the original NF.II in service during 1942 the leading Allied night fighter of the war.

AI radar was not the only night fighting aid to be introduced in the early stages of the war. During 1940 numbers of Douglas DB-7 Havocs were received from the United States, and a small proportion of these had the glazed bomber nose replaced by solid noses housing batteries of eight or 12 machine guns plus AI radar sets. The first squadron to be equipped with Havoc night fighters was No 85, which began operations with the type in February 1940 and continued until the following September.

In fact, No 85 was the only squadron to use the Havoc as a normal night fighter, and other examples were used in less conventional ways. In December 1940 No 93 Squadron was formed to use another variant of the Havoc, which was fitted with a device known as the Long Aerial Mine, or alternatively by the code name Pandora. This consisted of 2000 ft (610 m) of piano wire, at the end of which was attached a small explosive charge. Wire and charge were either trailed behind the aircraft, or released on small parachutes. In fact it created more of a hazard to the parent aircraft than to any opponent.

The dangers of the Pandora led to its abandonment, and instead Havocs were switched to Turbinlite squadrons. The idea behind these units was that the Havocs, or Bostons as some models were known, with 2,700,000,000-candlepower searchlights in the nose, would home in on hostile bombers, then switch on the searchlight to illuminate the target for accompanying Hurricanes to shoot down. No fewer than nine Turbinlite squadrons were formed in September 1942, with 70 Havocs modified to carry the searchlights, but by January 1943 only two hostile and one friendly aircraft had been successfully attacked using the system, while 17 Havocs had been lost in crashes, and the squadrons were disbanded.

Mosquito bombers with their crews preparing for a mission in February 1943

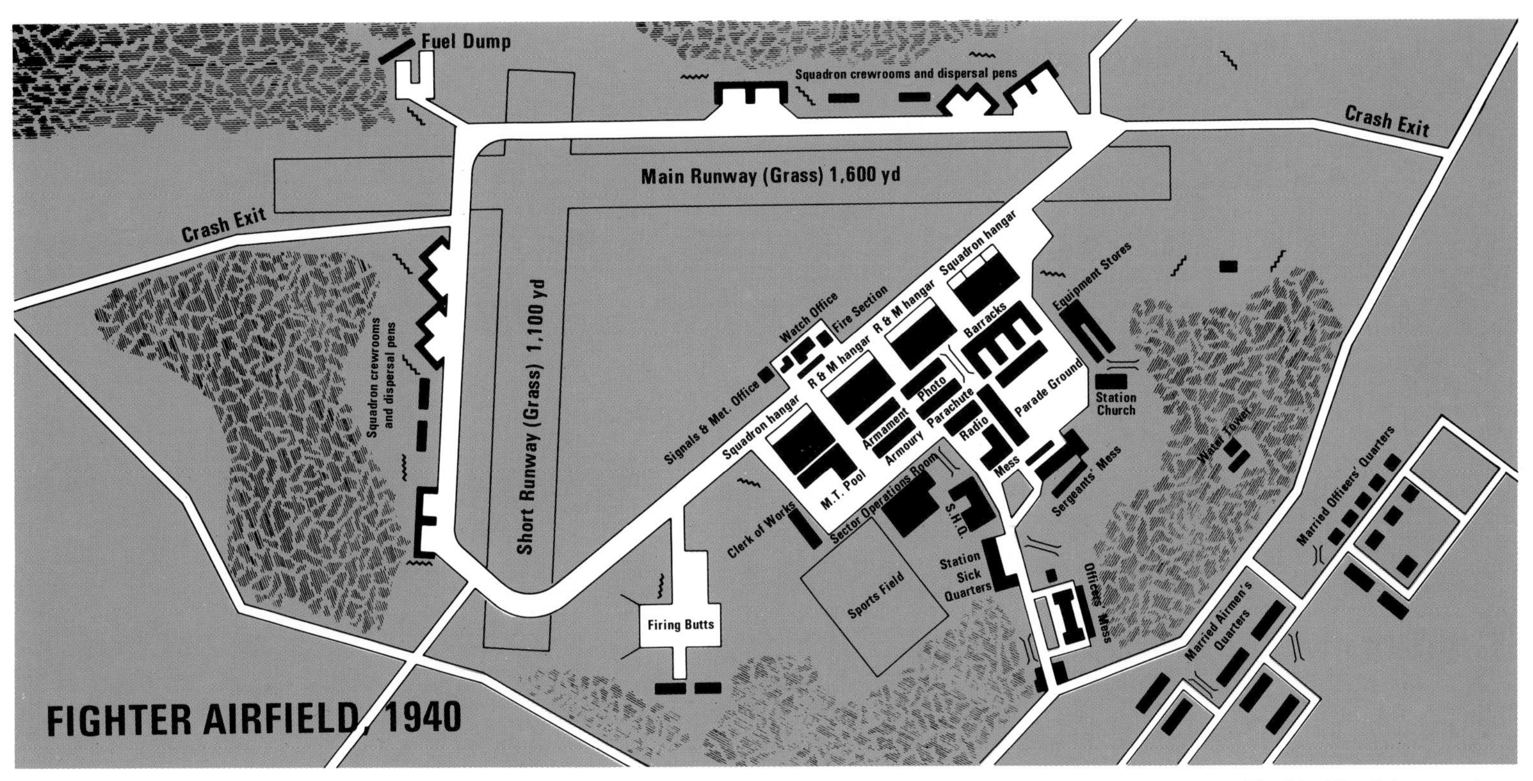

The Bristol Beaufighter proved an ideal vehicle for the early airborne interception radar equipment

An early example of the Douglas DB-7 imported from the United States and used both as a night fighter, under the name Havoc, and as a light bomber, in which role it was known as the Boston

A variety of inducements are offered to potential volunteers in the window of this recruiting office in the spring of 1941

FLY
RAF
CAN VOLUNTEER
ROYAL AIR FORCE
RECRUITING VISIT
THE R.A.F. WANTS
VOLUNTEER NOW!
ROYAL AIR FORCE
BRITAIN'S R.A.F.

THE BOMBING OFFENSIVE

KM S

The principal effect of the leaflet-dropping and anti-shipping raids that constituted Bomber Command's main activities during the early part of the war was to demonstrate the ineffectiveness of the equipment at its disposal. The bombers proved vulnerable to the German fighters, being inadequately armed and unprotected by armour or self-sealing fuel tanks; navigation by night was still a matter of star sights and uncertain radio beacons backing up dead reckoning; and systems were prone to malfunction or would seize up altogether in the extreme cold encountered at high altitudes, where the crews also became liable to frostbite and oxygen starvation. It was unsafe for the bombers to operate by day, while at night they had little chance of even finding their targets, let alone delivering their bombs accurately.

During the first eight months of the war the bombers were in any case held back from attacks on Germany. However, following the invasion of France and the German bombing of Rotterdam, while No 2 Group's Blenheims joined the attacks on German communications and troop concentrations, suffering losses almost as heavy as those of the French-based Blenheims and Battles, the first raids were mounted on targets in Germany.

THE BOMBING OFFENSIVE

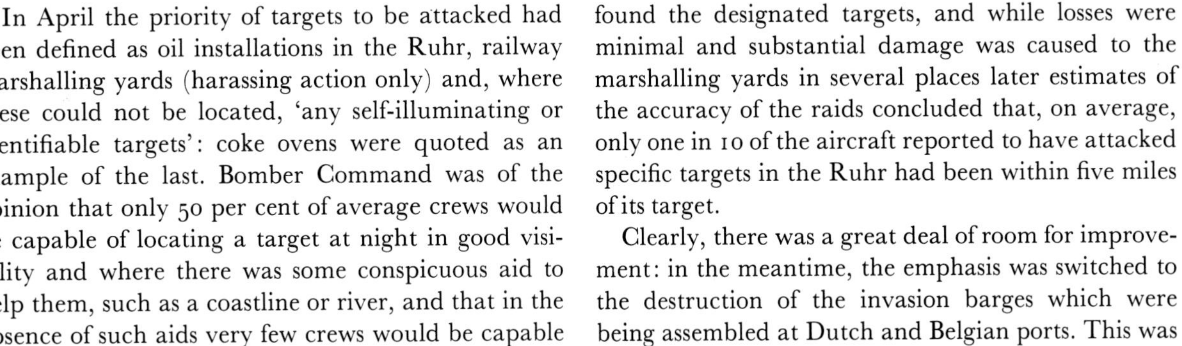

Previous page: Avro Lancasters of No 50 Squadron in formation

In April the priority of targets to be attacked had been defined as oil installations in the Ruhr, railway marshalling yards (harassing action only) and, where these could not be located, 'any self-illuminating or identifiable targets': coke ovens were quoted as an example of the last. Bomber Command was of the opinion that only 50 per cent of average crews would be capable of locating a target at night in good visibility and where there was some conspicuous aid to help them, such as a coastline or river, and that in the absence of such aids very few crews would be capable of finding it at all.

This opinion was borne out by the results of the first attack on the Ruhr oil refineries on the night of 15 May. Out of 78 Wellingtons, Whitleys and Hampdens of Nos 3, 4 and 5 Groups, only 24 claimed to have found the designated targets, and while losses were minimal and substantial damage was caused to the marshalling yards in several places later estimates of the accuracy of the raids concluded that, on average, only one in 10 of the aircraft reported to have attacked specific targets in the Ruhr had been within five miles of its target.

A camouflaged Fairey Battle on a French airfield in 1940. The crippling losses suffered by Battles and Blenheims in daylight raids in the early stages of the war were one of the factors behind the switch to the night bombing offensive

Clearly, there was a great deal of room for improvement: in the meantime, the emphasis was switched to the destruction of the invasion barges which were being assembled at Dutch and Belgian ports. This was accomplished much more effectively, and a raid on Berlin on 25 August also had satisfactory results, not in the negligible damage inflicted but in the subsequent switch of the German bomber offensive away from the Fighter Command bases to London and other cities.

By the end of 1940 it was becoming clear that precision bombing of industrial and military targets was possible, but only with very high loss rate for the crews involved. Moonlight and a readily identifiable target were essential, and to hit the target the bomber needed to fly straight and level for as much as 10 miles. Since important targets were likely to be well defended, such an approach was verging on the suicidal, and it was eventually decided that since most of the bombs would miss anyway, the answer lay in more extensive bombing of a whole area. At the same time there was a requirement for more effective bombs, and for more accurate methods of assessing the damage caused.

By this stage more effective bombers were beginning to arrive, though several promising designs were compromised to a greater or lesser extent by the terms of the original specification. The Short Stirling, for example, was built to meet a 1936 specification calling for a four-engined heavy bomber capable of 230 mph (370 km/h) at 15,000 ft (4572 m) with a range of at least 3000 miles (4827 km), a service ceiling of 28,000 ft (8534 m) with a 2000-lb (907-kg) bombload and all-round defensive armament. The overall limiting factor on the design, however, was the stipulation of a maximum wing span of 100 ft (31 m), to allow the new bomber to fit through the standard hangar door width.

The result was that the wings were of long chord with a corresponding low aspect ratio, in order to obtain the necessary area, so that performance at altitude was severely restricted and a fully loaded Stirling was pushed to get above 12,000 ft (3658 m). The tall undercarriage dictated by the high wing position made ground handling tricky, and the Stirling was very slow in climbing. The two-gun nose and dorsal turrets and four-guns in the tail formed a useful defensive armament, and at the time it entered service in August 1940 it was the RAF's only four-engined bomber. A divided bomb bay meant that the biggest bomb that could be carried was 4000 lb (1814 kg), but 24 500-lb (227-kg) bombs could be carried without using the auxiliary fuel tanks, and up to a total of 14,000 lb (6350 kg) over shorter ranges.

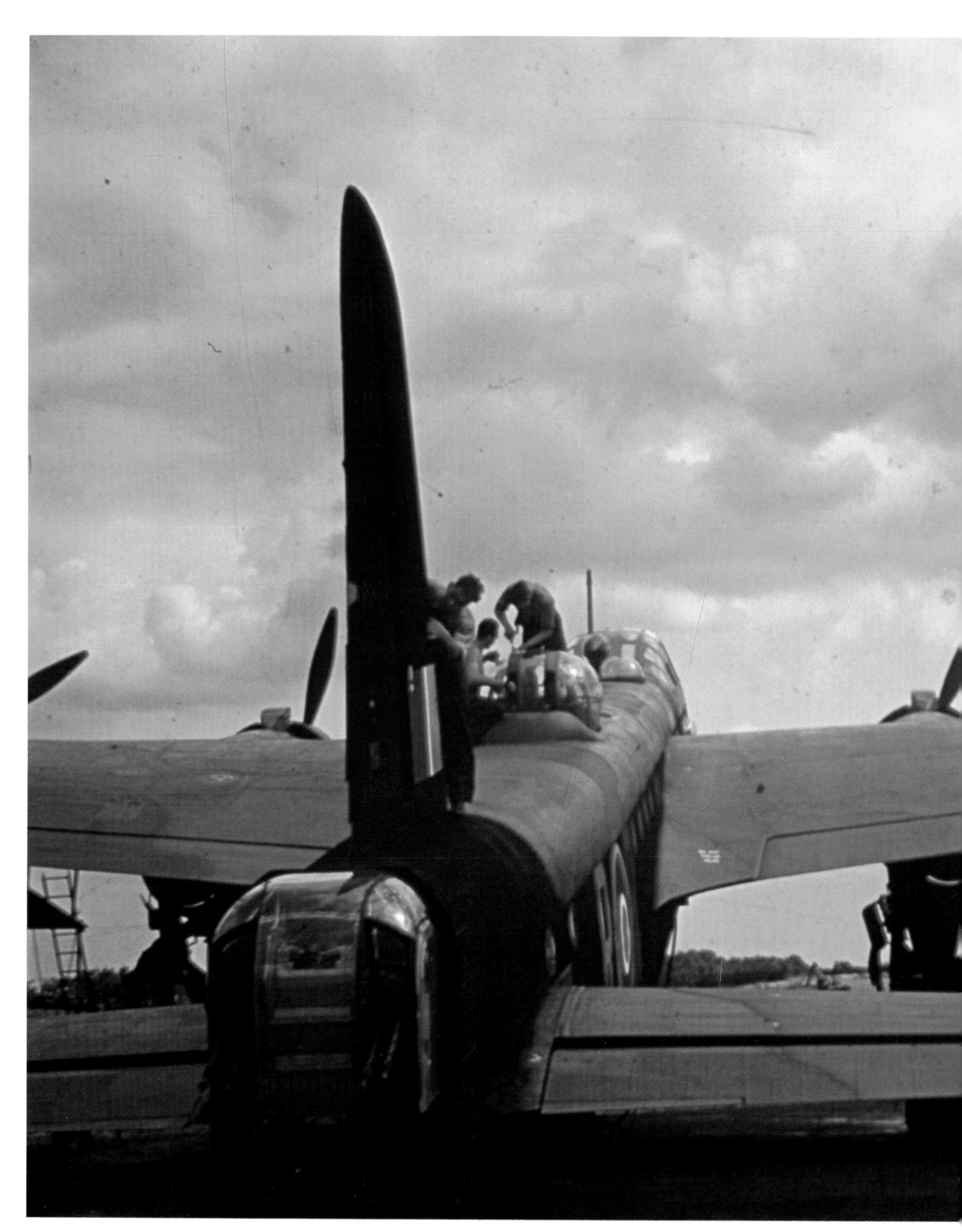

Ground crews at work on Short Stirlings of No 149 Squadron at RAF Mildenhall, late 1941. The Stirling was the principal heavy bomber in the early stages of the bombing offensive against Germany

The RAF's other four-engined bombers both began life as twin-engined types using the Rolls-Royce Vulture engine stipulated by another specification of 1936. The Avro Manchester actually entered service with this powerplant in November 1940, but this otherwise outstanding design was ruined by the completely unreliable engines, and production was abandoned after the first 200 or so had been completed.

The Handley Page design to the same specification was abandoned at an early stage, and the Vickers-Armstrong Warwick was redesigned to use Bristol Centaurus then Pratt & Whitney Double Wasp radials, but by the time the first production example was flown in May 1942 the design was out of date, and most Warwicks were used as transport, reconnaissance or air-sea rescue aircraft.

In the meantime, the original Handley Page twin-Vulture design had been enlarged to use four Merlin engines, and in this form the first prototype was flown in October 1939. By the time production examples were entering service alongside Manchesters in November 1940 the Halifax, as the new type was named, was armed with two-gun nose and four-gun tail turrets, plus a single Browning on each side of the beam. Halifaxes ultimately served in a variety of roles apart from night bombing, and in the Mediterranean and Far Eastern theatres as well as with Bomber Command in Europe.

Performance of the early Halifax models was not particularly impressive, but the installation of 1650-hp Bristol Hercules XVI sleeve-valve radials in the Mk III improved matters. The 1800-hp Hercules 100 fitted to the Mk VI from 1944 raised the maximum speed to 311 mph (501 km/h). Range with a 13,000-lb (5897-kg) bombload was 1077 miles (1734 km), and in 75,532 bombing sorties Bomber Command Halifaxes dropped a total of 227,610 tons (231,251,760 kg) of bombs. This represented more than twice the total weight delivered by Wellingtons in just under double the number of sorties, but the Halifax's totals were

more than doubled again by the most famous of all Bomber Command's aircraft, the Avro Lancaster.

The Lancaster was derived from the Manchester by a process similar to that which produced the Halifax, namely by replacing the two Vultures with four Merlins. Apart from the new wing centre sections demanded by the new powerplant, the basic Manchester airframe remained substantially unchanged, and many of the early Lancasters used original Manchester fuselages. Among the many attributes of the resulting bomber was an ability to deliver its bombs from a height of 20,000 ft, a much safer altitude than that of the Stirling, whose crews suffered many anxious minutes on bomb runs as the Lancasters and Halifaxes rained their bombs down from thousands of feet above. Another safety factor was the Lancaster's ability to stay airborne on only two engines, and to absorb substantial damage, and this was reflected in the type's low loss rate: while one Stirling was lost for every 41 tons (41,656 kg) of bombs dropped, and one Halifax for every 56 tons (56,896 kg), the average for the Lancaster was 132 tons (134,112 kg). One Lancaster managed 140 operational sorties, compared with an average for the type of around 20.

By January 1942 Bomber Command was a formidable organisation. No 1 Group had nine Wellington squadrons operational and one in reserve, while the other group principally equipped with Wellingtons, No 3, had 10 operational and one in reserve, as well as three squadrons operational with Stirlings. Most of the Wellingtons in service at this stage were Mk ICs, which dispensed with the ventral turret in favour of beam guns. Other later models of the Wellington included the Mks II, III and IV, powered by, respectively, Merlin, Hercules and Twin Wasp engines, while the last Bomber Command variant was the Hercules-powered Mk X.

No 2 Group at this stage was still mainly equipped with Blenheims, which equipped six of its operational squadrons. Another was already operational with

A Lancaster prepares to take off on a night mission from that familiar wartime location, 'somewhere in England'

Inset: The Lancaster's forerunner, the Avro Manchester, was the victim of its unsuccessful Vulture engines. This example belonged to No 207 Squadron

Bostons, another was in the process of conversion, while a third was converting to Mosquito Mk IVs. The Boston was the basic light bomber version of the Douglas DB-7, also used by Fighter Command as a night fighter with the name Havoc. The B.IV was the first main bomber version of the De Havilland Mosquito, the most versatile RAF aircraft of the war and Bomber Command's fastest bomber for nearly 10 years.

Originally built as a private venture light bomber, the Mosquito was designed to be built entirely of wood, following established De Havilland practice, and with two Merlin engines predicted performance was so good that it was proposed that no armament need be carried. Despite the radical nature of this proposal a small number were ordered, starting with prototype fighter, bomber and photographic reconnaissance versions. The PR versions were the first in service, closely followed by bomber conversions produced while the initial B.IV production bomber variant was awaited. The latter entered service in May 1942 with No 2 Group, and eventually proved able to carry a bomb load of 4000 lb (1814 kg) – compared with a designed load of 1000 lb (454 kg) – over a range of 1450 miles (2335 km). Performance was up to that envisaged, with a top speed of 380 mph (612 km) enabling the type to carry out unescorted daylight raids.

Meanwhile, No 4 Group in January 1942 was composed of three Halifax, six Whitley and two Wellington squadrons among its operational squadrons. No 5 Group at this time was equipped mainly with Hampdens, which were used by seven of its operational and one reserve squadrons, while one had received Lancasters and three were still using Manchesters.

During 1941 the emphasis in the bombing offensive had changed. At the beginning of the year oil plants were still regarded as the primary target, but as it became clear that there was simply no means by which these could be destroyed in precision attacks – most of the time the weather alone made it impossible for the bomber crews to find them – doubts grew about the value of the offensive. In August it was disclosed that only one in four of those crews who claimed to have found their target had done so, and it was still rare for bombs to fall within five miles of the target.

The appointment of Air Marshal Arthur T Harris as Commander-in-Chief, Bomber Command, on 22 February 1942 marked the completion of the swing towards area bombing tactics. Bomber Command's objective had been redefined a few days earlier to make the undermining of civilian morale its principal task; and by this time the first 100 or so bombers had been equipped with a new navigation aid known as Gee. Gee was based on the use of three radio transmitters broadcasting a complex train of pulses which could be deciphered using a special receiver in the aircraft in conjunction with a specially prepared map of Europe to enable the position to be fixed to within about six miles at a range of 400 miles from the transmitter by measuring the time intervals between the signals.

Gee was first used operationally in March 1942, with the suitably equipped aircraft using flares and incendiary bombs to light the target – Essen – for the main force to follow. Initial results were disappointing, with only one bomb in 20 falling within five miles of the town. An attack the same month on Lübeck proved more satisfactory, largely because it was easier to find, and the next step was to mount raids involving bigger concentrations of bombers than the 234 launched against Lübeck.

The idea of sending a thousand bombers over Germany in a single night was suggested by Harris to his deputy, Air Vice-Marshal Robert Saundby, in May 1942, and although the normal front-line strength of Bomber Command at this point was no more than 400 aircraft, it was calculated that by using all available bombers, including those currently used by Coastal Command and training units, and by bringing all unserviceable machines up to operational condition, it might just be possible to assemble the magic number. In the event the use of Coastal Command aircraft was vetoed by the Admiralty, which had operational control of the command, but a final total of 940 were finally prepared for the raid.

Above: Mosquitos proved able to carry out unescorted raids and were used for photographic reconnaissance and by the Pathfinder Force. The B.IV was the first bomber variant

Originally scheduled for the night of 27/28 May, the massive raid had to be postponed for three days because of the weather, but in the interval more aircraft became available, so that on the night of 30 May a total of 1046 bombers took off to bomb Cologne. Some 910 of the bombers reached the target, and 39 failed to return; 600 acres of the old city were destroyed, 45,000 people rendered homeless and 469 killed out of a total of around 5000 casualties.

The main result of the raid, however, was to win support for a continued and expanded campaign of area bombing. At that point there was little prospect of attacking Germany in any other way, and with more and bigger bombers Harris was predicting the imminent conclusion of the war as despair spread through Germany. Nothing of the sort was to happen of course, but more and bigger bombers were what Bomber Command got. Between February 1942 and March 1943 the number of operational aircraft with the command increased from around 500 to over 1000.

At the same time, the techniques employed were becoming more sophisticated. By November 1942 jamming equipment known as Mandrel was being used to jam German Freya early warning radar, and another system code-named Tinsel had been introduced to jam radio communications between German night fighters and their ground controllers. These devices were fitted to two bombers in each squadron, and used to screen the others. Another countermeasure introduced alongside Mandrel and Tinsel in July 1943 was Window, which consisted of quantities of aluminium foil strips dropped by the bombers to confuse the Würzburg tracking radar operators by producing hosts of bogus echoes.

The electronic war continued to the end of the war, as new developments in the German detection equipment provoked new countermeasures. In the meantime, improving the bombers' navigational accuracy was just as vital as protecting them from the German night fighters. In this respect the system known as H2S was a great improvement, being self-contained within the aircraft and providing the operator on board with a representation of the terrain below. At the same time, another system of ground control named Oboe became available. Oboe used a pair of ground transmitters generating signals which were amplified and returned by a transponder on the aircraft, allowing the ground controllers to obtain an exact fix on its positions and control its approach to the target by radio instructions.

The use of Oboe was limited to controlling one aircraft at a time, and its maximum range was about 270 miles (434 km) with the aircraft flying at 28,000 ft (8534 m) because directional signals were used and range was limited by the curvature of the earth. Consequently, the Pathfinder Force, otherwise No 8 Group, Bomber Command, was formed in August 1942 to use the radar aids to illuminate the target with incendiaries. This finally allowed targets in the Ruhr, previously shielded by an all but impenetrable haze of smog, to be located with some accuracy.

For a year, starting in March 1943, Bomber Command carried out a concerted campaign, starting with the Ruhr, switching to Hamburg in July and turning towards Berlin itself in November. Spring brought a change of emphasis during the preliminaries to the Allied landings in Normandy. Thereafter, as the German defences crumbled, the might of Bomber Command was directed against German towns and cities, culminating in the notorious raid on Dresden, when a night raid by more than 800 RAF bombers was followed during the day by 400 USAAF bombers, resulting in the complete destruction of 1600 acres of the city and the death of many thousands of its inhabitants and the refugees who were there.

By the end of the war in Europe, when Bomber Command had reached a strength of 84 operational squadrons, it was equipped with over 2000 aircraft, including 1282 Lancasters, 475 Halifaxes and 265 Mosquitos. In addition, 13 Bomber Support squadrons in No 100 Group disposed of another 260 aircraft, including small numbers of Fortress and Liberator types received from the United States. The latter were only two of the American types used by Bomber Command; others included the Mitchell and Ventura, and all found more extensive employment with other arms of the RAF.

There had also been a number of developments of the basic heavy bombers for special purposes. Among the best known of these were the 'Dambuster' Lancasters equipped with the Barnes Wallis bouncing bombs to attack the Möhne and Eder dams. Lancasters were also the vehicle for the delivery of the biggest conventional (as opposed to nuclear) bombs of the war. These were the 10-ton (10,160 kg) Grand Slams, also developed by Barnes Wallis, and first used against the Bielefeld viaduct in March 1945.

The Tallboy bombs which preceded the Grand Slams were comparative lightweights at 12,000 lb (5443 kg). These were completely different from the earlier bombs of that weight, which were simply 4000-lb (1814-kg) bombs bolted together in threes: the essence of the Tallboy was that it was designed to penetrate deep into the surface after reaching supersonic speeds. The Tallboys proved particularly useful against otherwise impenetrable targets. First used against the Saumur railway tunnel in June 1944, they scored subsequent successes against U-Boat pens and,

perhaps most spectacularly, against the battleship *Tirpitz* in its Norwegian anchorage the following November. A total of 854 Tallboys and 41 Grand Slams were delivered before the end of the war in Europe, adding further laurels to the career of the Lancaster, the only bomber of the time capable of both accommodating and lifting the giant weapons.

Another aspect of the bomber offensive was the provision of the fighter escorts in the later stages of the war. At the start of the bombing offensive no RAF fighter had the necessary range to accompany the bombers on their raids, which was one of the main reasons why they were forced to switch to night attacks. At first this provided protection, but the later generations of German night fighters, equipped with such devices as Naxos, which allowed them to home in on the H2S mapping radar, and Flensburg, which added a new dimension to the electronic war by fixing the bombers' Monica tail warning radar designed to alert the crews that a fighter was on their tail, necessitated a continuing counter-effort. One result was the use of Mosquito night fighters of No 100 Group as specialised electronic support aircraft. One device which these used was known as Perfectos, and used the German fighters' own identification radars, fitted to enable the ground controllers to differentiate between friendly and hostile aircraft, to guide the pilot to an interception. The simple counter to Perfectos was for the German pilots to switch off their identification equipment, but this had the drawback of making the controllers' task infinitely more difficult.

Fortresses, Stirlings and Halifaxes were equipped with ever more extensive jamming equipment. Biggest of all was Jostle, which jammed the entire frequency range of the German control transmissions. Piperack was another jamming device carried by the bigger bomber support aircraft, and was designed to jam the night fighters' radar rather than its communications.

The overall success of the bombing offensive has been a source of controversy ever since it ended in 1945. Its effects on war production have been debated endlessly, with the conclusion drawn depending on the interpretation of the figures: that production increased throughout the war is indisputable, but what it would have been without the interference of Bomber Command can only be a matter for conjecture. Again, defence against the bombers certainly diverted a good deal of the German war effort from other areas, but only at the cost of 67,000 air crew killed and 4200 wounded on operational service and at the expense of an estimated seven per cent of the British national war effort. What it did prove, not for the first time, was that aerial bombardment strengthens the resolve of the civilian population rather than destroying its morale. Perhaps the most lasting testimony to its validity is in the fantastic cost of rebuilding Europe afterwards, and in the historic cities such as Dresden which were lost to future generations forever.

Left: One of a batch of 20 Boeing B-17Cs supplied to the RAF in 1941 and used briefly by No 91 Squadron. The B-17 was named the Fortress in RAF service

Above: A North American Mitchell of No 28 Squadron, one of the medium bomber squadrons of No 2 Group, returns from a daylight raid over northern France

TACTICAL SUPPORT

Following the collapse of Allied resistance in France in May 1940 there was little need for army co-operation work in Europe. The Lysander squadrons that had crossed the Channel to support the BEF were switched to coastal patrol duties on their return, and in December a new Army Co-operation Command was formed. It was in North Africa, however, where the army launched its first offensive of the war in the same month, that the new methods of tactical support were to be developed.

The Mediterranean theatre was something of a backwater until the Italians joined the war in June 1940. During the next year the Italian forces in East Africa were driven out, and Iraq and Syria were secured. The Italians were also driven out of Cyrenaica (eastern Libya) between December 1940 and February 1941, but the arrival of Rommel in North Africa during the latter month presaged a new phase of the war in the desert. While Axis forces blitzkrieged their way through the Balkans and Greece (Crete fell in May), the island of Malta, of vital strategic importance because of its position in the middle of the sea lane between Sicily and the North African coast, came under siege, and Rommel pushed the British and Commonwealth forces back to the frontier of Egypt.

It was only in the summer of 1941 that the obsolescent aircraft that had formed the Middle East Command's strength at the start of the war began to be replaced, and even then much of the new equipment consisted of American aircraft supplied under Lend-Lease. Another problem was one of organisation. Middle East Command at the beginning of 1941 covered a vast area, stretching from British East Africa to the Balkans and from Libya to Iraq, and not only its own organisation but also its communications with the forces on the ground were in need of thorough overhaul.

Following the consolidation of the position in East Africa and Iraq and Syria, and the withdrawal from Greece, this was carried out in the second half of 1941. East Africa was left to South African units, and No 8 Squadron in Aden continued to use Blenheims and Vincents for antisubmarine patrols and internal security duties. Palestine and Transjordan were patrolled by two squadrons of Hurricanes plus a Fleet Air Arm squadron with Albacore fighters and Swordfish torpedo bombers, in addition to a Free French Morane-Saulnier 406 fighter squadron and another Free French flight of Blenheims. Three squadrons, one each of Audaxes, Hurricanes and Vincents, were based in Iraq, and Malta was the base for three squadrons each of Blenheims and Hurricanes, another of Martin Marylands, part of a Wellington squadron and further Fleet Air Arm units.

Air Headquarters, Egypt, included two transport squadrons equipped with Bristol Bombays and Douglas DC-2s plus a General Reconnaissance Unit with Wellingtons, another squadron acting as an Operational Training Unit for Maryland crews and Hurricane squadrons for air defence. No 205 Group in the Suez Canal zone had five long-range bomber squadrons with Wellingtons, and No 201 Group based at Alexandria was equipped with a variety of types for air-sea rescue and reconnaissance.

At the same time, in November 1941, the forward units acting in support of the ground forces were reconstituted as Air Headquarters, Western Desert. In addition to the HQ squadrons with a variety of transport, reconnaissance, fighter and light bomber types, there were three fighter and two light bomber wings, the former with Hurricanes and Tomahawks and the latter using Blenheims and Marylands. An important aspect of these wings was that they were intended to be fully mobile, but while the necessary transport vehicles were awaited a new system of co-operation with the ground forces was evolved.

Above: A Martin Baltimore lands at Accra after crossing the Atlantic on its way to join the RAF in the North African desert
Previous page: A De Havilland Mosquito Mk 3 stands at its dispersal point

It had been recognised by this stage that the first requirement for effective air support was local air superiority, and the fighters were able to achieve this under RAF control. Support of the ground forces was a more complicated matter however: since the desert war was one of rapid movement, it was often difficult for the air controllers to know the precise location of the Allied lines. To overcome this problem, a new system of Air Support Controls was established to co-ordinate requests for air support and relay these to the airfields, to the aircraft in the air and to the Air Headquarters. At the same time, air-ground co-ordination was improved by new rules for indicating targets and establishing bomb lines ahead of the Allied troops. Finally, to back up the front-line units, the maintenance situation was improved by the establishment of a new system for the retrieval and repair of damaged aircraft, the supply of aircraft and spares and the storage of supplies.

Consequently, the air forces were able to intensify their efforts against the Luftwaffe. At night the Wellingtons attacked the German airfields and the supply convoys crossing the Mediterranean, and during the day the light bombers struck at the forward air bases. The see-saw battles that continued until the turning point at Alamein in August 1942 were accompanied by a steady improvement in both the quantity and the quality of the air support, and the development of specialised ground-attack aircraft.

Early equipment of the squadrons in North Africa had included a number of American designs. Several of the South African Air Force squadrons were equipped with Curtiss Mohawks and Tomahawks, the latter also being used by RAF and Royal Australian Air Force units. These corresponded to the USAAC's P-36 and P-40, the latter being an improved version with an Allison V-1710 in-line engine in place of the earlier model's Double Wasp or Cyclone radial. Original armament was six machine guns, but as later models, named Kittyhawk in RAF service, became available the standard armament was reduced to four wing-mounted 0.5-in Brownings plus a 500-lb (227-kg) bomb under the fuselage or smaller bombs under the wings.

A number of American light bomber types were also used by the RAF in the desert war. The Martin Maryland, like the Douglas Boston, was originally ordered by France, and along with other aircraft in production for the French after May 1940 was taken over by the RAF. The Martin Baltimore was a redesigned Maryland built to RAF specifications, and after early models were delivered with manually aimed Vickers K guns in the dorsal position a Boulton Paul powered turret was installed in the Mk III and a Martin turret in the Mk IV. For close-support work the Baltimore also had a battery of ventral machine guns; two Vickers K guns were standard but some had four or six guns firing downward to the rear as well as four wing-mounted guns, and the bombload of 2000 lb (907 kg) remained the same as that of the Maryland.

Martin Maryland attack bombers serving with the Desert Air Force

Hurricane IIDs with 40-mm anti-tank cannon under their wings

The original armament of the Hurricane was also increased for the ground-attack role, and after the Mk IIB had introduced 12.303-in Brownings, the Mk IIC was fitted with four 20-mm Hispano cannon, both versions being equipped to carry a 250-lb (113-kg) bomb under each wing. A more specialised variant was the Mk IID, which carried a 40-mm cannon under each wing specifically to attack tanks, and later examples designated Mk IV and V were fitted with wings that could carry cannon, bombs, drop tanks or four 60-lb (27-kg) rockets each.

Meanwhile, the siege of Malta was intensified. In the first four months of 1942 some 10,000 tons (10,160,000 kg) of bombs had been dropped on the island, before early May brought the arrival of Spitfire reinforcements and the withdrawal of the bulk of the German bomber force from Sicily. However, while the assault lasted the Axis convoys were able to reach Tripoli, and in June Rommel began a new advance.

At this point the front was still west of Gazala, where it had stabilised at the end of Operation Crusader in February. In May the fighting was renewed and, after turning the Allied line, Rommel was able to drive forward, pushing back the Eighth Army 400 miles (644 km) in two weeks. A remarkable feature of this retreat was the preservation of the fighting force relatively intact, which in the case of the RAF squadrons was a result of the preparation of landing grounds at intervals all the way back to the frontier. The squadrons were divided into two parts, leapfrogging backwards over each other, cleaning out the supplies as they went and not leaving each base until the enemy was within 20 miles (32 km) or so – a distance judged approximately by the sight of their own bombs bursting. At the same time, the advancing German forces were kept under constant air bombardment.

By the beginning of July the advance had been halted at the defensive line at Alamein, while the aircraft kept up their attacks. The Baltimore and Boston light bombers had by now displaced the heavy Wellingtons from the Canal Zone: the former, escorted by Kittyhawks, carried out daylight attacks while Spitfires maintained air superiority and the Hurricane fighter bombers sought out their own targets, and at night the Wellingtons attacked Tobruk, now a German base, from their new bases in Palestine, refuelling in the Canal Zone en route.

In June and July the Wellingtons were joined in Palestine by Nos 159 and 160 Squadrons, on their way to India with Liberator B.IIs. Coastal Command had earlier equipped several squadrons with Liberators, and the B.II was the first bomber version to serve with the RAF. Powered by four Twin Wasp radials and armed with quadruple 0.303-in Brownings in Boulton Paul tail and dorsal turrets, plus single hand-aimed weapons of the same calibre in the nose and on each side of the waist, the Liberator B.II could carry 5000 lb (2268 kg) of bombs over a range of 2100 miles (3379 km). They were thus able to attack the principal Axis supply port of Benghazi, in Libya, previously a regular target for the Wellingtons, direct from their base in Palestine, and were retained in Palestine until the autumn for that purpose.

Between the consolidation of the Alamein line in July and the Allied Operation Torch landings in Morocco and Algeria in November, the various groups of RAF Middle East helped to seal the fate of the Afrika Korps, preventing supplies reaching the German and Italian armies, making concerted attacks impossible and maintaining the defence of Malta. During the pursuit of the Axis forces across Libya they kept up the work of harassing the enemy columns.

The desert war was far from over, but Rommel's ultimate defeat was now only a matter of time. In the meantime, the grand strategy for the defeat of the Axis had to be decided, and in January 1943 Churchill and Roosevelt met in Casablanca to work out the immediate objectives. It was decided to invade Sicily, since an invasion across the English Channel was not practicable during the new year.

For the RAF, this meant a new organisation to integrate the strategic bomber, tactical support and coastal formations with the growing American air strength in the Mediterranean theatre. The result was the Mediterranean Air Command, composed of RAF, Commonwealth and USAAF elements and subdivided into a series of subordinate commands. The bulk of the new force was divided between RAF Middle East and the Northwest African Air Forces, but there were also Air Headquarters at Gibraltar and Malta as well as the Mediterranean Air Transport Service, with two USAAF squadrons of Dakotas and No 216 Group, whose seven squadrons, including two South African Air Force units, operated various transport and communications types.

At the start of the invasion of Sicily in July 1943, Air Headquarters, Malta comprised a total of six squadrons of Spitfires, including one of the SAAF, three of Beaufighters and one of Mosquitos, plus a squadron each of Baltimores and Wellingtons. At Gibraltar there were two squadrons each of Hudsons and Catalinas, along with another of Wellingtons and detachments of Beaufighters and Spitfires.

Under RAF Middle East Headquarters came three special squadrons, one equipped with Liberators and Halifaxes used to supply resistance fighters in Greece, Albania and Yugoslavia, another using Wellingtons and Blenheims for radar calibration, as well as the occasional bombing raid, while the third had Spitfires and Hurricanes for photographic reconnaissance. No 201 Group continued in its coastal and maritime reconnaissance role, its four RAF, one Greek, two SAAF, two Royal Australian Air Force and two Fleet Air Arm squadrons using Beaufighters, Baltimores, Blenheims, Wellingtons, Hudsons, Walruses and Swordfishes. The US Ninth Air Force also came under RAF Middle East, its 20 squadrons of Liberators serving alongside one RAF and one RAAF squadrons of Halifaxes, though other units were attached to Northwest African Tactical Air Force and Troop Carrier Command.

Other components of RAF Middle East were Air Headquarters in the Levant, where one squadron of Hurricanes was based; Iraq and Persia, with a squadron of Blenheims and a detachment of Hurricanes; East Africa, which extended as far as South Africa and deployed four squadrons of Catalinas for anti-submarine patrols over the Indian Ocean; and British Forces Aden, where a flight of Catalinas and a squadron of Blenheims were based. Finally, there was Air Defences, Eastern Mediterranean, whose 16 squadrons of Hurricanes included three SAAF and one RAAF, and which also incorporated two squadrons of Beaufighters and one of Spitfires.

Northwest African Air Forces were again composed of various formations devoted to different functions. The biggest of these, Northwest African Tactical Air Force, was further divided between the Desert Air Force, the US XII Air Support Command and the Tactical Bomber Force. Other components of the NWAAF were the Strategic Air Force, Troop Carrier Command, Coastal Air Force and the Photographic Reconnaissance Wing.

RAF, SAAF, RAAF and Royal Canadian Air

The Duke of Gloucester at Ismailia, with a Consolidated Liberator behind him. The long-range Liberator was the principal heavy bomber in the North African campaign

Force units formed the Desert Air Force, which included 17 squadrons of Spitfires, six of Kittyhawks, and one each of Hurricanes and Mosquitos, alongside six USAAF squadrons of Warhawks. The Tactical Bomber Force included eight squadrons of Boston and Baltimore light bombers, of which three were SAAF, plus a squadron each of Spitfires and Hurricanes for tactical reconnaissance. XII Air Support Command, the third component of the Desert Air Force consisted of 16 squadrons of Mustangs, Warhawks (as Kittyhawks were known in American service) and Spitfires.

The Strategic Air Force was primarily an American affair, including 36 squadrons of Flying Fortress, Mitchell and Marauder bombers plus 12 squadrons of Lightning and Warhawk fighters. There were, however, a further six RAF and three RCAF squadrons equipped with Wellingtons. The Coastal Air Force, on the other hand, had a majority of RAF squadrons, which included six of Beaufighters, three of Hurricanes, two each of Blenheims, Wellingtons, Hudsons, Spitfires and Walrus air-sea rescue machines, plus one each of Marauders and Baltimores. The American contribution comprised two squadrons of Liberators, six of Airacobras and three of Spitfires.

The two remaining components of the Northwest African Air Forces, Troop Carrier Command and the Photographic Reconnaissance Wing, were predominantly American. The former had a squadron of RAF Albemarles and a detachment of Halifaxes, but the 27 squadrons of USAAF Dakotas formed its major carrying capacity. The smaller PR Wing included a squadron of Spitfires and detachments of Mosquitos, along with two squadrons of Lightnings and one of Flying Fortresses.

Following the successful invasion of Sicily and the subsequent landings in Italy itself, and then the long struggle to defeat the German armies after the armistice with Italy in September 1943, there was a rationalisation of these various commands. The subordinate formations under Middle East Command continued to be based on their geographical locations, but the Northwest African Air Forces merged with Mediterranean Air Command. The result was a similar division of responsibilities, but the various arms now consisted of the Mediterranean Allied Tactical, Strategic and Coastal Air Forces, the Desert Air Force continuing to form the major part of the tactical air force.

At the same time, June 1944 brought the formation of a new command, the Balkan Air Force, which was established to assist the growing resistance movement in occupied Greece and, particularly, Yugoslavia. The equipment of the new arm, a representative selection of the various types equipping the main forces in the theatre, enabled it to carry out similar tasks: bombing attacks on supply and communications facilities, anti-shipping strikes, the disruption of German landings on the Adriatic islands, the dropping and landing of arms and other supplies to the resistance forces and fighter-bomber attacks on targets of opportunity such as troop trains. A particularly notable achievement of the Balkan Air Force was the large-scale evacuation of wounded partisans, some 11,000 of whom were flown out from improvised airstrips to hospitals in Italy. In addition, another 2500 people were landed in occupied territory, and a total of 16,400 tons (16,662,400 kg) of supplies were delivered.

At the same time as preparations were under way in the Mediterranean for the invasion of Sicily and Italy, the longer-range planning for the inevitable cross-Channel invasion was also under way in Britain. Almost as soon as the German daylight bombing raids had ceased in the autumn of 1940, Fighter Command had begun a programme of raids over the continent. Among the operations carried out were those code-named Circus, involving heavily escorted groups of light bombers whose real purpose was to provoke a response from the German fighter defences. A handful of Blenheims might be accompanied by 20 or more squadrons of fighters, but just as the Hurricanes had been outclassed by improved models of the Bf 109, so that they were used first for low-level escort of the bombers, and then more and more as fighter-bombers, so the Spitfires began to meet superior opposition in the form of the Focke-Wulf Fw 190.

As a result, heavy losses began to be suffered both from the sparse but effective fighter opposition and from the fierce anti-aircraft fire that was normally encountered around any important target. The same applied to the Roadstead anti-shipping strikes that were another regular feature of Fighter Command operations in 1941, and while the Rhubarb strikes (carried out by one or two fighters at low level) generally managed to evade interception they were more useful as training exercises for the pilots than for the damage caused.

At the same time, the German tactics had changed to include similar operations, and a degree of specialisation in fighter design was obviously called for. The Spitfire V that had been introduced in March 1941 with 1440-hp Merlin 45 or 50 engines was fitted with A, B or C wings able to carry alternative armament of eight .303-in Brownings, four Brownings and two 20-mm cannon, or four cannon. The Mk VB was the standard fighter version in 1941–42, and while the specialised Mk VII high-altitude version and Mk VIII all-purpose version were under development the Mk VI, with a pressurised cabin, was produced as an interim measure. At the same time, the necessity to combat the Fw 190 led to the installation of the more powerful 60-series Merlin engine in a basic Mk V airframe.

The resulting Spitfire IX was ultimately built in greater numbers than any other variant except the Mk V, and to equip it for different roles it was given extended wingtips for enhanced high-altitude performance, or clipped wings for fast low-level flight. Similar modifications were made to produce low-

A Martin Marauder, another of the medium bombers to serve with the Allied air forces in the North African and Mediterranean theatres

altitude Mk Vs, but by this time an even better low-level fighter had appeared in the form of the Hawker Typhoon. In fact, it was some time before the Typhoon's abilities in this role were recognised, and trouble with the powerplant, the Napier Sabre, delayed its acceptance, while poor altitude performance almost caused its withdrawal from service. By 1942, however, it had demonstrated its ability to catch low-flying Fw 190s which had taken to low-level sweeps on Rhubarb lines. The Typhoon was also used along with the twin-engined Westland Whirlwind for attacks on Channel shipping, but while the Whirlwind only equipped two squadrons and was replaced by 1943, the Typhoon went on to become a highly successful ground-attack fighter, carrying 1000-lb (454-kg) bombs or eight 3-in rockets as well as its normal armament of four 20-mm cannon.

Another new fighter of 1941 which excelled at low altitudes was the North American Mustang, originally ordered in 1940 by the purchasing mission to the United States. The original Mustang I was used by 14 squadrons of Army Co-operation Command, but later models, which replaced the Mk I's Allison engine with a Packard-built Merlin showed a dramatic improvement in performance at all levels, and shone particularly as a long-range bomber escort. The Mk Is were used mainly for tactical reconnaissance and Rhubarb sweeps over the continent.

By June 1943 the strength of Fighter Command had reached 102 squadrons, though 20 of these were tactical support units temporarily allocated to the command. The main fighter strength included 43 squadrons of Spitfires, 14 of Typhoons, 10 of Beaufighters, 10 of Mosquitos, two of Whirlwinds and one each of Defiants and Bostons. The army support component included 13 squadrons of Mustangs, one each of Tomahawks and Hurricanes and five of Taylorcraft Auster III Air Observation Post machines. The Austers operated in close co-operation with army units for liaison and artillery observation, flying from any convenient field, and often crewed by army pilots and observers.

In August 1942 Fighter Command fought its biggest single battle of the war in support of the raid on Dieppe. Hurricane fighter-bombers, along with the light bombers of No 2 Group, supported the troops carrying out the landing by laying smoke screens and attacking defensive strongpoints, while the Spitfire squadrons maintained a defensive umbrella overhead. During the day of 19 August 2617 sorties were flown by RAF aircraft, of which 106 were lost. Some high claims were made for the number of Luftwaffe aircraft destroyed, though it was calculated after the war that German losses amounted to only 48, with a further 24 damaged. They were kept away from the landing forces with great success, but at the same time some other lessons were learned. One was the futility of firing aircraft guns against concrete emplacements, another was the need for more comprehensive control of the aircraft.

Accordingly, towards the end of 1943 a new command was formed for the support of the D-Day landings. Named the 2nd Tactical Air Force, the new organisation incorporated the various elements of Army Support Command, the light bombers of No 2 Group, Bomber Command and many of Fighter Command's squadrons. In addition, there were heavy bombers and transports adapted for paratroop dropping and glider towing to transport the airborne forces.

In the months leading up to the invasion, too, there was heated debate about the use of the strategic bomber forces. Bomber Command and US Eighth Air Force commanders wanted to continue undistracted with the strategic offensive which many of them considered would make the landings unnecessary: the men responsible for planning the operation, on the other hand, wanted a concerted offensive against enemy communications which would simultaneously help to convince the defending forces that the invasion would be carried out in the Calais region, help to draw labour away from the construction of defences, and prevent reinforcements reaching the landing area in Normandy.

In the end, the tasks the air forces were called on to carry out were summarised under five headings: maintaining air superiority; continuous reconnaissance of enemy dispositions and movements; the disruption of communications and supply lines;

500-lb (227-kg) bombs about to be loaded on a Hawker Typhoon IB of No 175 Squadron, 2nd Tactical Air Force

A newly built Handley Page Halifax II on a test flight

offensive strikes against enemy naval forces; and airlift of the airborne forces. For the actual assault phase, the objectives were the protection of the invasion fleets; neutralising the beaches where the troops would land; protecting the beaches after the landings; and disrupting ,enemy movements and communications during the landings.

To this end, the 2nd TAF disposed of an impressive 96 squadrons, including Commonwealth units, divided between six groups. No 38 Group, with four squadrons of Albemarles, four of Stirlings and two of Halifaxes, along with No 46 Group's five squadrons of Dakotas, were allocated to paratroop dropping and glider towing. No 2 Group of light bombers included two squadrons of Bostons, four of Mitchells and six of Mosquitos. The two fighter-bomber groups, Nos 83 and 84, together comprised 28 squadrons of Spitfires, 18 of Typhoons and 11 of Mustangs. No 85 Group, whose task was air defence of the overseas base, had four squadrons of Spitfires, two of the Tempest development of the Typhoon, and six of Mosquito night fighters. This group operated under the command of No 11 Group, now part of Air Defence of Great Britain and the other component of the Allied Expeditionary Air Force which had been created to control the 2nd TAF, which in turn was responsible to ADGB for night operations and 2nd TAF for day.

During the D-Day landings and the subsequent fighting north towards Germany the two principal tasks of the 2nd TAF resolved themselves into reconnaissance and close support, directing attacks against tanks, troop concentrations and other targets at the request of the ground commanders. Air superiority was the prerequisite for the success of these operations, which were helped by the destruction of bridges and the disruption of transport and communications. The rocket-firing fighters proved particularly useful in destroying trains and armour.

As the Allied armies advanced across Europe, another threat was posed to Air Defence of Great Britain by the new flying bombs. The launching sites had been subject to attacks since late 1943, but new ramps were erected almost as quickly as old ones were destroyed, and after the flying bomb offensive opened on 12 June the number of launches mounted rapidly. Consequently, the fighters of No 11 Group were called on to intercept the V-1s, as they became known. The most successful interceptors of V-1s were the Hawker Tempests, and another new fighter used for the task was the Gloster Meteor, the world's first fully operational jet aircraft, which equipped a single squadron in the summer of 1944.

The pushing back of the German lines eventually ended the flying bomb offensive, as it was no longer possible for them to reach England, but at the same time the V-2 rockets began to be directed against London. There was no hope of intercepting these once they had been launched, and bomb-carrying Spitfires were used to attack their launching sites in Holland instead.

In October 1944 ADGB reverted to its name of Fighter Command, leaving the 2nd TAF to continue its support of the Allied armies' advance towards Berlin. The fighter-bombers extended their activities to include attacks on enemy headquarters buildings, and their success in the tactical support role was vividly illustrated during the German offensive in the Ardennes in December 1944. Between 16 December, when the offensive began, and 23 December the German advance averaged 12 miles a day. During that week, however, the weather had prevented operational flying: on 24 December, when the weather lifted sufficiently to allow nearly 600 sorties to be flown, the advance was slowed dramatically, and by the following day it had come to a halt.

Left: Pilot and liaison officer with an Auster Aerial Observation Post aircraft

Below: Bostons of the 2nd Tactical Air Force prepare for take-off

THE WAR AT SEA

During the Second World War, as in the First, one of Germany's most dangerous offensives was directed against the shipping on which Britain's war effort depended. When war was declared German U-Boats, pocket battleships and commerce raiders were already at sea, and within hours the *U-30* had sunk the liner *Athenia* 200 miles (322 km) west of the Hebrides. This was a mistake: the U-Boats were under orders to attack military targets only, and *U-30*'s commander had mistaken the liner for a troop ship. Nevertheless, it was an early reminder of the dangers to Britain's supply lines, and it hastened the introduction of convoys.

Unfortunately, there were few ships available to escort the convoys, and they were of limited endurance, so that at first the convoys could only be escorted for the first 300 miles (483 km) of the west-bound journey, after which they dispersed to make their own way. Incoming convoys normally had an armed merchant cruiser as escort as far as the 300-mile (483-km) limit, with a naval escort joining them at that point.

It had been found during the First World War that aircraft, with their extended view, were a great deterrent to submarines in the vicinity of convoys, but the problem in 1939 was the lack of long-range patrol aircraft. The Fleet Air Arm had been completely separated from the RAF shortly before the outbreak of war, but there were too few carriers to accompany the convoys. Also the land-based aircraft of Coastal Command were limited to a radius of about 500 miles (800 km) from the coast. For the U-Boat threat to be contained, there were many requirements, starting with longer-range aircraft, but also including a more efficient patrol system and, most important of all in the long run, effective methods of locating and attacking submarines.

By 1939 there were three new types on order for Coastal Command. One of these was the Blackburn Botha, designed to a 1935 specification and ordered off the drawing board in 1936. Unfortunately, the Botha's entry into service in the summer of 1940 revealed it to be both underpowered and otherwise unsuitable for the task, and it was used only briefly for patrols over the North Sea before being relegated to training. Another failure was the Saunders-Roe Lerwick, a twin-engined flying boat which proved unstable in the air and was cancelled after only 21 had been built.

Fortunately, the third of the new types was a success. The Bristol Beaufort avoided the problems of the Botha by replacing the specified Bristol Perseus engines with the more powerful Taurus. Between November 1939 and June 1940 Beauforts replaced the two squadrons of Vildebeests, previously Coastal Command's only torpedo bombers, and equipped one new squadron as well as replacing Ansons in two others. The type also served with two squadrons in the Mediterranean, but its true potential was reached with the redesigned Beaufighter.

The Beaufighter combined the wings and tail of the Beaufort with a new, slimmer fuselage housing a two-man crew instead of the original four, and Bristol Hercules engines. Early Beaufighters achieved great success as radar-equipped night fighters, and with the 1595-hp Hercules XVI engines the Mk IVC succeeded the Mk Ic in 1942. The Mk IVC added a torpedo-carrying capability to the 1500-mile (2415-km) range of the earlier version, and provided a useful extension of Coastal Command's patrol range.

The early stages of the U-Boat campaign were actually reasonably well contained: the convoy routes were switched away from the southwestern approach to the English Channel to the northwest. By the end of March 1940, when the U-Boats were recalled for the Norwegian invasion, 199 merchant ships had been sunk, but so had 18 U-Boats, and the British naval blockade was proving successful in preventing supplies reaching Germany.

However, the occupation of Norway in April and then of France in May and June changed the situation dramatically in Germany's favour. Now long-range

Previous page: A Short Sunderland of Coastal Command escorts an Atlantic convoy

Left: A Bristol Beaufort II based on Malta for strikes against Axis shipping in the Mediterranean

Below: The Saunders-Roe Lerwick was intended for large-scale service with Coastal Command, but proved unstable and production was abandoned at an early stage

Focke-Wulf Fw 200 Condor aircraft could use bases in Norway to attack shipping in the northern waters, and the U-Boats were provided with new bases in the Bay of Biscay, allowing them much easier access to the mid-Atlantic. During the second half of 1940 losses of merchant shipping reached an average of 450,000 tons (457,200,000 kg) a month, nearly 60 per cent of which was sunk by U-Boats, while the Condors sank 12 per cent and mines and surface ships were responsible for the remainder.

At this point there was a suggestion that Coastal Command should follow the Fleet Air Arm in becoming part of the Royal Navy, but neither service was in favour of this, and the solution was found in the creation of combined headquarters, with the command remaining part of the RAF but being placed under the operational control of the Admiralty from April 1941. No 15 Group headquarters were located at Liverpool alongside the new Western Naval Command, and a new group, No 19, was formed at Plymouth to co-operate with the naval command there.

Early in 1941 a squadron of Hudsons and another of Sunderlands were based in Iceland to extend the patrol area in the mid-Atlantic, and a similar force was based in Liberia to patrol the sealanes off western Africa. Nevertheless, the rate of sinkings was already exceeding the rate of replacement, and during the first few months of 1941 it rose again, reaching a total of 644,000 tons (654,304,000 kg) in April, with nearly half of the total being accounted for by aircraft.

At the same time, there were some encouraging developments. On 6 April a suicidal attack by a Beaufort of No 22 Squadron succeeded in severely damaging the battle-cruiser *Gneisenau* in the harbour at Brest. Towards the end of May a Catalina flying boat of No 209 Squadron succeeded in locating the battleship *Bismarck* in the mid-Atlantic, and the ensuing air and sea operations resulted in the sinking of another serious threat. Equally significant was the loss to the German Navy in March of three of the most experienced U-Boat commanders.

Evasive routing of the convoys and the gradual extension of air patrols and escort protection for convoys, coupled with the sinking or containment of the principal German surface ships resulted in a dramatic reduction in the number of merchant vessels sunk in June and July. This was partly a result of the strengthening of No 15 Group's Atlantic patrols in the western approaches, following the introduction of Bomber Command Blenheims on North Sea patrol duties, while the use of catapult-armed merchantmen, carrying a single Hurricane which could be launched to fight off the Condors whose reconnaissance was vital to the success of the U-Boats also helped. After an increase in the figures for August and September, the remainder of the year saw dramatic falls in losses in the Atlantic, though this was mainly a result of the U-Boats being switched to operations in the Mediterranean.

The new year, with the entry of the United States into the war, brought an alarming increase in losses. Convoys were not immediately adopted by the Americans, and U-Boats operating off the north-eastern coast of the United States were able to sink 505 ships in the area before the introduction of convoys at the end of June. The U-Boats then changed their area of operations again, to the 'black gaps' in the mid-Atlantic, where no air cover could be provided. Throughout 1942 Allied losses averaged 650,000 tons (660, 400,000 kg) per month, still short of the 800,000 tons (812,800,000 kg) the Germans considered necessary to achieve a decisive victory, but also well ahead of the rate of replacement. Moreover, US commitments in the Pacific, the demands for convoys to the northern Russian ports, and the requirements of the convoys for the Torch landings in North Africa were combining to stretch the escort forces still further.

Consequently, the beginning of 1943 marked the crucial stage in the battle for the Atlantic sealanes. The U-Boat commanders had many months of experience behind them, and with the benefit of intelligence provided by the cryptanalysts, who had succeeded in breaking the convoy cypher, they were able to mount a concerted attack on the March convoys. In that month 39 U-Boats intercepted two convoys bound for Britain, sinking a total of 21 ships. This success marked the high point in the battle as far as Germany was concerned. In the following months a combination of new aircraft and equipment was to turn the battle decisively in the Allies' favour.

One of the most important innovations was the

Liberators of No 220 Squadron based at Lagens in the Azores for anti-submarine patrols in the South Atlantic

development of centimetric ASV (air-to-surface-vessel) radar, which enabled aircraft fitted with the equipment to locate surfaced submarines at night. The first ASV Mk III radar sets, converted from H2S equipment intended for bombers but diverted to Coastal Command when it was realised that the U-Boats were equipped with receivers that could detect the emissions of the earlier, and less useful, radar transmitters, were installed in Liberators towards the end of 1942.

Another development, designed to improve the efficiency of the earlier ASV sets, was giving the patrol aircraft a means of illuminating U-Boats which had been detected. Within about three-quarters of a mile (one and a fifth km) of the target the U-Boat became indistinguishable from the general reflections from the sea surface. The answer came in the fairly obvious form of a powerful searchlight – named the Leigh Light after its inventor – which could be switched on to light up the submarine once the radar set had tracked it to the limit of its detection range. The first installations were tried as early as January 1941, but its service introduction was delayed as a result of the unfortunate Turbinlite programme for night fighters. The latter was given priority, although its diffused beam was quite different from the concentrated beam of the Leigh Light, and it was only after the Turbinlite's unsuitability had been demonstrated that full-scale trials of the Leigh Light were carried out.

These were made by Wellingtons of No 172 Squadron in June 1942 in the Bay of Biscay, and proved resoundingly successful. The result was that the U-Boats were forced to travel submerged through the Bay of Biscay on their way to and from their bases, severely limiting the amount of time they could spend on active patrol in the Atlantic.

A Martin PBM-3B Mariner, one of a small batch supplied to the RAF. The dome above the cockpit houses search radar equipment

Having detected a submarine using radar or Leigh Light, an aircraft then needed an effective weapon with which to attack it. The use of bombs against submarines had quickly proved unproductive, and the standard Mk VII depth charge was not much better. By 1942 the Mk VIII depth charge had been introduced: filled with Torpex instead of the less powerful Amatol and with a pistol that could be set to detonate it at a depth of 25 ft (7.6 m) this proved much more effective.

Finally, the provision of Very Long Range Liberators early in 1943 enabled the gaps in the Atlantic patrols to be filled, and immediately the rate of Allied losses began to decline, while the sinkings of U-Boats showed a dramatic increase. Two months after the March convoys had been intercepted with such success, another convoy battle took place in the Atlantic. This time, however, with more escorts available and aircraft using the new radar, the U-Boats were on the receiving end and eight of the 12 attacking submarines were sunk.

Within the next three months the U-Boat battle was all but over. The waters of the Bay of Biscay became so dangerous that the submarines themselves were forced to travel in convoys with air escorts, but combined operations by aircraft and naval forces caused the abandonment of this tactic too. The introduction of snorkels to allow the U-Boats to recharge their batteries without surfacing reduced the chances of detection, but at the cost of inhibiting their freedom of movement. Acoustic torpedoes introduced at the beginning of 1943 were soon countered by escorts towing noise making devices behind them to decoy the homing mechanism. The revolutionary new Walther propulsion system, using hydrogen peroxide fuel in a closed cycle steam turbine to free the vessel of the need for constant recharging of batteries, raised as many problems as it solved.

By this stage, in any case, Germany no longer had the capacity to man enough submarines. The demands of the war effort were such that the new boats being built at the rate of 25–30 per month in 1943 could only be crewed by transferring officers from the army and air force. The U-Boats continued to be dangerous, switching tactics and changing their areas of operation repeatedly, but the strength of the naval escorts was steadily increased by the provision of merchant ships converted into temporary aircraft carriers, and in conjunction with the land-based patrol aircraft and the Sunderland and Catalina flying boats they kept the U-Boats on the defensive for the remainder of the war.

The battle against the U-Boats was not Coastal Command's only responsibility during the war. From June 1941 the Photographic Reconnaissance Unit, using Spitfires and Mosquitos equipped with high-resolution cameras in heated installations to prevent them freezing up, had been part of Coastal Command, and by October 1942 there were five squadrons employed on this work. Their tasks included photographing targets after bombing raids to assess damage, searching out radar transmitters, providing detailed pictures of the landing sites in the preliminary planning of the Allied invasions, monitoring shipping movements in German-controlled ports and, following the invasion of France, providing detailed pictures of enemy positions that were about to be attacked.

Another vital aspect of Coastal Command operations was the air-sea rescue service of aircrew in home waters. The peak year for this activity was 1943, when 1648 individuals were retrieved, 708 of them in the third quarter. Regular meteorological flights were made to chart conditions in the upper atmosphere and over the North Sea and Atlantic, gaining information of the highest importance in planning air raids and, most notably, the D-Day landings.

A Short Sunderland I, original version of one of the mainstays of Coastal Command's battle against the U-Boats

THE WAR IN THE FAR EAST

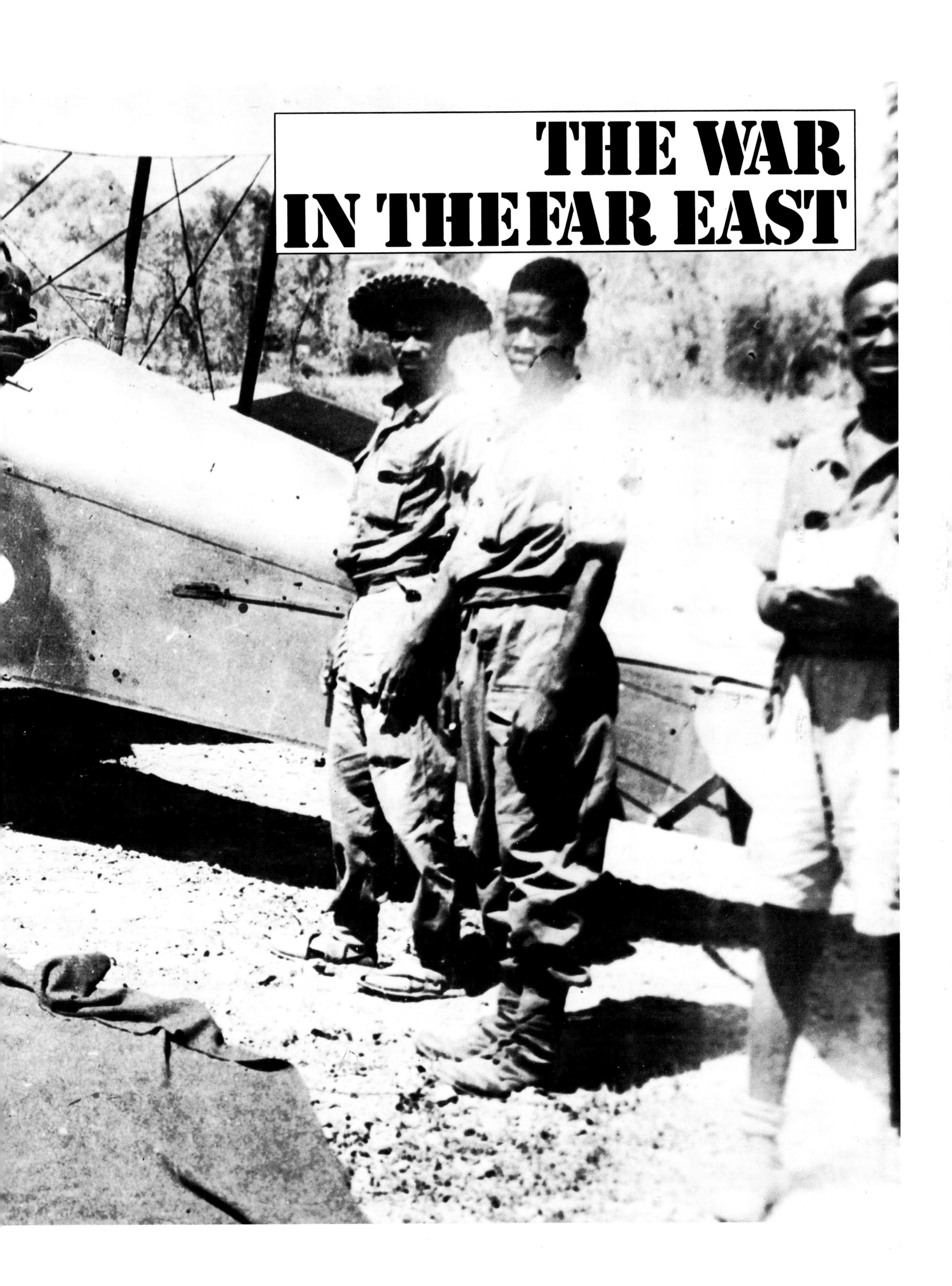

At the start of the war in Europe the island of Singapore, Britain's main naval base in the Far East, was defended by a battery of 15-in guns and a few squadrons of obsolete aircraft. Trenchard's suggestion 15 years earlier that the RAF should provide the main defence of the island had been rejected, and the guns were installed because it was anticipated that Singapore would be attacked from the sea. During 1940, however, it was realised that the Royal Navy was not in a position to do much about the island's defence, and the RAF was given responsibility for protecting it against a possible Japanese invasion.

Unfortunately, by this stage the RAF was itself overstretched. In October 1940 it was estimated that 566 aircraft was the minimum first-line strength required to defend the British interests in the Far East: by the beginning of December 1941 the total had reached 362, of which 233 were serviceable, and almost all of which were thoroughly outmoded. In Singapore itself there were four squadrons of Blenheims and two of Vildebeests. The Sunderland squadron had been transferred, first to Ceylon and then to Egypt, and in its place there was a single squadron of Catalina flying boats. The Royal Australian Air Force provided two squadrons of Hudsons and two of Brewster Buffalos: the latter, ordered from the United States in 1939, had been rejected for service in Europe, and was shipped out to the Far East, where it was thought at least capable of dealing with Japanese opposition. One RAF and one RNZAF squadron were also equipped with Buffalos by December 1941.

Elsewhere in the Far East the situation was hardly any better. Ceylon (Sri Lanka) was still defended by a single squadron equipped with a mixture of Vildebeests and Seal floatplanes. In Burma there was another squadron of Buffalos and a few Blenheims of No 60 Squadron, most of whose aircraft were at Singapore. Hong Kong and Borneo had no air defences. However the Japanese, widely believed to have no worth-while combat aircraft, had been at war with

Previous page: A wounded East African soldier waits for evacuation by air during the retreat from Burma

China since 1937 and actually had some extremely capable combat machines, including the Zero, one of the best fighters in the world at that time.

Under orders to refrain from provoking Japanese aggression, the squadrons at Singapore could do little. Hudsons spotted Japanese convoys 300 miles (483 km) off the coast of the Malayan peninsula on 29 November 1941, but contact was lost when the weather impeded further reconnaissance flights. By the time the news of the attack on Pearl Harbor reached Singapore the Japanese landings had already begun.

During the following weeks British resistance was crushed. Six squadrons had been deployed in the Malayan peninsula, but most of their aircraft were destroyed on the ground. The remainder could do little to halt the air raids on Singapore itself, and by the end of January 1942 most of the surviving aircraft had been withdrawn to Sumatra, where the story was repeated, and the final remnants continued the fight on Java, until there were simply no more aircraft left to fly. In Burma, the Blenheims of No 60 Squadron and the Buffalos of No 67 were aided by an American Volunteer Group squadron flying Curtiss P-40s, and these were reinforced shortly after the Japanese invasion by another squadron of Blenheims and a number of Hurricanes to replace the outclassed Buffalos. These put up a strong resistance to the Japanese air attacks on Rangoon, and managed to cover the early stages of the army's withdrawal, but by April most of the surviving aircraft had been withdrawn for the defence of India itself.

In the event, apart from an attack on Ceylon in April 1942, the defenders of India had little to do. No air raids were mounted against Calcutta until December, and the arrival of a flight of radar-equipped Beaufighters in January 1943 soon halted these: six out of nine bombers on two separate raids were shot down, and no more were attempted. Consequently, there was time to re-organise the air forces, and to plan the ultimate defeat of the Japanese in Southeast Asia.

Hurricane and Thunderbolt, air support for the ground forces in Southeast Asia

The first requirement as far as the air forces were concerned was a massive increase in strength, and a corresponding provision of new airfields. A programme of airfield building begun at the end of March 1942 made slow progress at first, but by the end of the year five were operational, while another 850 or so single-runway and fair-weather landing strips were in use. By November 1943 the number of airfields with two runways had risen to 275, apart from further landing strips.

At the same time, the number of squadrons showed a steady increase, with new fighter, dive-bomber and reconnaissance units bringing the number up to 26 in March, compared with only five in the whole of India three months earlier. The dive-bomber squadrons were equipped with the Vultee Vengeance, the RAF's only purpose-built dive-bomber, which had been ordered from the American firm in 1940 after the German Stukas had proved so impressive in the early German blitzkriegs. By the time deliveries were under way the shortcomings of the dive-bomber – its vulnerability and the need for fighter escorts to allow it to operate without interference – had been realised, and the type was used operationally only in the Far East.

In support of the subsequent Allied offensives in Burma, however, the Vengeance gave extremely useful service. One technique developed in Burma involved the use of bombs with delayed-action fuses, set for varying intervals so that bombs continued to explode at unpredictable times after the attack was over. When the ground troops were preparing an attack, the bombs would be dropped without any fuse at all, allowing the men on the ground to advance in safety while the defenders waited for the explosions to start. The Vengeance was armed with five 0.5-in machine guns, two in each wing and one in the rear of the two-man cockpit, and could carry up to 2000 lb (907 kg) of bombs.

One reason for the ability of the Vengeances and Hurricanes, which carried out most of the ground-support attacks, to operate with relative freedom was the withdrawal of the bulk of the Japanese air forces from Burma to help counter American pressure on other fronts after May 1943. In October of that year Allied air superiority over Burma was further strengthened by the arrival of the first Spitfire squadrons, whose first task was to stop the Japanese photographic reconnaissance flights, whose interception had proved beyond the ability of the Hurricanes. Photo-reconnaissance Spitfires had begun operations over the Burma front the previous November.

Meanwhile, reconnaissance over the Bay of Bengal was carried out by Catalinas and Hudsons based in Ceylon. The Consolidated Catalina was used in substantial numbers by the RAF, and the type really came into its own in the Pacific and Indian Ocean, where its range of over 3000 miles (4830 km) in the reconnaissance role came in particularly useful. Blenheims previously employed for coastal patrols were replaced by Beauforts during 1942, and by February 1943 the first squadron of Liberators was supplementing their efforts. The arrival of the Liberator squadrons had been delayed when they were pressed into service in the Middle East to support the Alamein offensive, and it was not until September 1943 that the first Liberator bombing unit was able to begin operations. Two squadrons of Wellingtons had begun operations the previous year, though one of these was engaged on supply dropping and training with airborne forces for several months after its arrival. Another achievement during 1942 was the creation of a network of radar stations along the Burmese border, with control centres at Calcutta and other places, including the main forward base at Imphal. With the establishment of maintenance and supply depots, the air force was rapidly reaching a useful operational capability.

During the second half of 1942 Japanese defences and British preparedness were tested by the first Arakan offensive along the coastal strip of Burma. A planned element of this offensive had been the capture of the Japanese airfield on the island of Akyab – one of the locations where the retreating British air elements had regrouped briefly during the retreat from Burma the year before – but the necessary landing craft for the operation had been retained in the Middle East. By September the land advance had already begun. Ultimately, the offensive proved beyond the capacity of the available force, but pressure from above meant that the retreat was postponed until the end of March 1943, when the position finally became untenable.

At the same time as the Arakan offensive was becoming bogged down, another operation of novel and daring conception was mounted behind the Japanese lines to the north. This was the famous expedition of the Chindits – officially the Long-Range Penetration Brigade – led by Colonel Orde Wingate, and deriving their familiar name from operations on the Japanese side of the Chindwin river. Each of the eight columns which made up the 3000-strong force was accompanied by an RAF radio detachment: the basis of Wingate's plan was that they should be able to operate independently in Japanese-occupied territory, relying on supplies dropped by air. The Dakotas of No 31 Squadron and the Hudsons of No 194 were responsible for carrying out the supply drops and it was this element of the operation which was to prove most significant for the future campaign in Burma.

During the remainder of 1943 the build-up of strength continued, with the ageing Blenheims replaced by Hurricanes for close support work and several squadrons of Spitfires arriving. In November a new command was formed for Southeast Asia, and the air forces of Britain and the United States were combined in the Eastern Air Command, which was in turn divided into strategic, tactical and troop carrying arms.

By mid-1944 the headquarters element of Eastern Air Command comprised a fighter wing with two squadrons of Spitfires and one of Beaufighters, plus a photographic reconnaissance force including two RAF

Right: Bristol Blenheim IVL, with long-range fuel tanks in the wings

squadrons, one with Spitfires and the other with Mosquitos and Mitchells, plus three American squadrons using Lightnings, Warhawks and Liberators. The Strategic Air Force included four USAAF squadrons of Liberators and another of Mitchells, while the RAF contributed three squadrons of Liberators, one of Wellingtons and an air-sea rescue squadron with Vickers Warwicks, the latter type having been designed originally as a replacement for the Warwick but serving instead in the rescue role.

The 3rd Tactical Air Force combined a substantial American Transport and long-range bomber group, the latter including four squadrons of Mitchells. The seven squadrons of Dakotas included in 3rd TAF, however, were later absorbed into the Combat Cargo Task Force which replaced the Troop Carrying Command which had been dissolved in June with the start of the monsoon season. Also included in the CCTF were eight RAF transport squadrons equipped with Dakotas. The remainder of 3rd TAF comprised RAF and Indian Air Force elements, amounting to 11 squadrons of Hurricanes, five of Spitfires, two using Vengeance dive-bombers and one with Beaufighters, plus an American squadron with Lockheed Lightnings.

Eastern Air Command itself formed part of Southeast Asia Command. Apart from the two special-duty squadrons using Hudsons, Liberators and Catalinas to infiltrate and supply agents and special forces operating behind enemy lines in occupied Malaya and Sumatra, the remainder of the overall command comprised the reconnaissance force of maritime patrol types based on Ceylon, plus the nine squadrons responsible for defending the rest of India.

By this stage, Eastern Air Command already had some impressive achievements to its credit. In November 1943, simultaneously with the formation of the new organisation, a second offensive had begun in Arakan. This time concerted bombing of Japanese airfields, supply centres and other strategic targets by the Wellingtons and Liberators formed the background to the advance into Burma, and the Japanese forces were thwarted in their attempts to cut off and destroy the 7th Indian Division as a result of regular supplies being flown in to the beleaguered force. Vengeances were able to provide protection from Japanese air attack and dive-bombing, allowing a relief force to re-open the lines of communication so that the Japanese were defeated in Arakan by the end of February 1944.

By this time, however, the Japanese had launched their own offensive, and by 9 March Imphal was under attack. The latter was reinforced at great speed with the aid of Dakotas diverted from other duties, but then supplying the strengthened garrison became a problem. The heavy American C-46 Commandos, normally used for supplying the armies in China, were too much for the runways at Imphal, which were in any case frequently rendered unusable by the weather: only by piling up stocks at alternative points then ferrying them in when the weather relented could even minimal rations for the defenders be maintained.

Finally, the road to Imphal was opened again on 22 June. By this time the transports had flown in

12,561 men and nearly 19,000 tons (19,304,000 kg) of supplies, and 13,000 casualties and 43,000 non-combatants had been airlifted out. Both aircrew and ground handlers were near collapse by this stage, and Imphal could not have held out much longer. Without the airlift it could not have survived at all.

The same was true at Kohima, where the defenders were besieged in a much smaller area following the start of the Japanese attack on 4 April. Kohima's position on an exposed ridge surrounded by mountains made the dropping of supplies extremely difficult. Nevertheless, while Hurricane and Vengeance attacks helped keep the attackers at bay, the Dakotas flew in regularly, dropping their cargoes from as low as 200 ft (61 m) above the ridge in order to minimise the risk of missing a position no more than a few thousand square yards in area. Fortunately for the defenders, the siege lasted only 13 days before relief arrived.

While the battles of Imphal and Kohima were raging, the Chindits were mounting a new and much more ambitious expedition. This time a force of 10,000 was to be flown deep into occupied territory by glider, while a further 2000 infiltrated the area on foot. The initial airborne element was to be transported in 80 gliders towed two at a time by Dakotas: these were to prepare landing grounds for the remainder to be flown in.

There were considerable casualties during the first phase, when a number of tow ropes broke and several gliders crashed: in fact, only 35 of the 61 gliders that took off on the first night reached their target. However, most of the Chindits were flown in by Dakota, and the various columns were kept supplied by air, while their casualties were flown out in light liaison aircraft and the RAF officers attached to each column were able to call in and direct bombing support. The exact value of the operation is difficult to assess: by the beginning of July the Japanese were in retreat after the defeats at Imphal and Kohima, and it has been claimed that the effort needed to support the Chindits could have been better used in those battles. On the other hand, the disruption caused by the Long-Range Penetration forces was certainly regarded as serious by the Japanese themselves, and in view of the narrowness of the margin of victory in the main battles, may have been decisive.

In any case, the air support was crucial to the success of the Allied cause, not only in the Arakan and on the central front, but also in support of the Chinese forces, under General Joseph Stillwell, which were

fighting their way down from North Burma. During the remainder of the campaign in Burma, which resumed in November after the rains had passed, RAF units achieved a high degree of specialisation in their support of the ground advance.

The strategic offensive continued, with attacks by the Liberators, which had finally replaced the last of the Wellingtons, being concentrated on the Burma-Siam railway which formed the principal Japanese supply route. Eventually raids were commonly carried out on targets more than 2000 miles (3220 km) from the Liberators' bases, and the introduction of the Azon guided bomb enabled many bridges to be destroyed. This comprised a standard 1000-lb (454-kg) bomb fitted with a radio receiver, steerable fins and a flare for tracking, so that an operator aboard the launch aircraft could guide it to its target.

The coastal patrol squadrons, meanwhile, were beginning to concentrate their efforts on the destruction of shipping off the Burmese coast, supplementing direct attacks with the laying of mines as far afield as Singapore. The photographic reconnaissance units, meanwhile, enabled detailed maps of the whole theatre to be compiled.

The most important aspect of the air contribution, however, was in direct support of the advancing ground troops. Republic Thunderbolts had begun to supplement the older fighter-bombers, providing a dramatic increase in close-support firepower. The Thunderbolt could carry a maximum of 2500 lb (1134 kg) of bombs, with a typical load consisting of a single 1000-lb (454-kg) bomb under each wing and another of 500 lb (227 kg) under the fuselage, and was armed with eight 0.5-in machine guns. The standard tactic for the Thunderbolt was the cab-rank patrol developed by the original tactical air force in the Western Desert. In a neat reversal of the original battlefield use of aircraft, when they flew above the front lines signalling map references to the artillery batteries below, the cab-rank patrols would loiter in the vicinity of the ground battle, waiting to be called into action by a controller on the ground.

By this stage of the campaign, the degree of air superiority provided by the Allied fighters was so nearly absolute that even Liberators were used in close support operations, delivering their heavier weight of bombs against enemy strongpoints. At the same time, Hurricanes continued to be used for close support, supplemented by the Spitfires which now had little opposition in the air.

Most important of all, however, was the supply operation without which the entire campaign could not have been fought. The steadily increasing distance from the main supply bases in Northeastern India led to the construction of new airfields as the advance progressed, each airfield being able to forward supplies over a radius of 250 miles (403 km). In the final stages of the advance on Rangoon, in April 1945, airfields were constructed every 50 miles (80 km), to serve as the base for the next leg.

The Consolidated Catalina was used extensively in the Indian Ocean for coastal patrol and other duties

TRAINING AND TRANSPORT

The Royal Air Force reached a peak strength in personnel of 1,185,833 in July 1944, 10 times the corresponding number of only five years before. The number of aircraft on charge in 1945 was, at its peak, 55,469: of these 9200 were first-line machines, more than three times the total number on strength in 1939.

One of the principal problems involved in the massive expansion described by these figures was the training of aircrew. Some progress had been made since the beginning of rearmament in the mid-1930s by the formation of the RAF Volunteer Reserve, members of which were trained at civilian flying schools under contract with the Air Ministry. However, with a wartime production rate of aircraft planned to reach 2500 a month the Volunteer Reserve could hardly be regarded as more than a starting point.

The answer was provided in the form of the Empire – later Commonwealth – Air Training Scheme, under which many thousands of aircrew were trained. The scheme began operation in May 1940 with the first schools for the training of RAF pilots in Canada, and eventually there were a total of 92 such schools when the scheme reached its peak in 1943. The scheme was expanded to include further establishments in Australia, New Zealand, South Africa, Southern Rhodesia and India, as well as Egypt, India, the United States and the Bahamas.

To deal with the demand not only for aircrew but also for skilled men in no fewer than 350 different trades, Training Command was divided to form separate branches to deal with flying and technical training. The latter was responsible for schools teaching everything from chaplaincy to bomb disposal as well as supplying the trained staff to deal with the aircraft and their associated equipment. Of course maintenance became at once more difficult, as aircraft in much greater numbers were subject to war damage as well as normal wear and tear; more complex, because the aircraft themselves were more complex, and more urgent, because they were needed back with their squadrons as soon as possible.

To deal with these problems, Maintenance Command was formed in April 1938, and during the war its four groups were responsible for all the equipment used. No 40 Group, operating its own railways and goods yards to deal with a turnover of stores that reached well over 300,000 tons (3,048,000 kg) a month in 1944, provided the Aircraft Equipment Depots. These dealt in all forms of equipment except bombs, explosives, aviation fuel and oil, which were the responsibility of No 42 Group, whose turnover rose from 1,000,000 tons (1,016,000,000 kg) in 1943 to over 3,000,000 tons (3,048,000,000 kg) the following year. No 41 Group received the aircraft from factories, and after inspection and the installation of any additional equipment the new aircraft were delivered to squadron bases by pilots of the Air Transport Auxiliary.

Finally, No 43 Group was responsible for the repair of the aircraft and any other equipment. These were retrieved, either from their bases or from locations where they had crashed, by salvage units, and apart from the turnover in aircraft the Repair Depots turned out large numbers of repaired and reconditioned engines.

A substantial number of aircraft were damaged as a result of accidents during pilot training, and in consequence the training schedule was revised during the war, especially for pilots destined to fly the complex four-engined bombers. The average flying time on training before the war was 146 hours, after which pilots would receive operational training with an active squadron. During the war the squadrons were too preoccupied with operations to continue this system, and following the normal basic training of 50 hours on Tiger Moths or Miles Magisters, and a further 110 hours on Miles Masters, North American Harvards or Airspeed Oxfords, trainee pilots would then spend another 40 hours on operational types at an

Above: De Havilland Tiger Moth, used for elementary flying training

Previous page: Four student pilots brush up their formation flying skills in these Miles Master Mk IIIs

Operational Training Unit. The Harvard was the standard advanced trainer with the Commonwealth Air Training Plan, the Master was the other standard single-engined advanced trainer, and the twin-engined Oxford was flown by pilots intended for multi-engined operational types, superseding the Anson for this purpose.

Later in the war this syllabus was expanded using the facilities of the overseas training schools. By 1944 a Lancaster pilot could expect to spend the best part of two years in training. After two months at an aircrew reception centre or initial training wing, during which 12 hours would be spent on Tiger Moths for assessment of aptitude, the trainee would spend 30 weeks overseas, during which he would spend at least 60 hours on basic trainers, followed by 155 hours on an advanced trainer. Further training on return to Britain might comprise another 80 hours on advanced trainers, followed by 80 hours on an operational type, 40 hours on a multi-engined type at a Heavy Conversion Unit, and a final 12 hours on a Lancaster at finishing school.

In the early stages of the war heavy bombers normally carried two pilots, but the demand was such that in March 1942 this was reduced to one. At the same time, his job was made easier by the addition of an automatic pilot, and a flight engineer was introduced who was also trained to land the aircraft in an emergency. The tasks of the other crew members were also revised. The observer became the navigator, and since he would be occupied with the new navigational equipment, bomb-aiming was taken over by another member of the crew who would also act as front gunner. The previous requirement for all air gunners to be trained as radio operators was also dropped: only one air gunner in each crew was also a radio operator, and others were gunners only.

A tenth home command was formed during the war.

Left: North American Harvards were among the most widely used trainers of the war years

Below: The RAF's first monoplane trainer, the Miles Magister entered service in 1937. This example is preserved by the Shuttleworth Trust

Ferry Command came into being in July 1941, succeeding the Atlantic Ferry Organisation. The latter was inaugurated in 1940 in order to speed up the delivery of new aircraft from the United States. The first aircraft used in what was a highly ambitious scheme for that time were Lockheed Hudsons, whose journey from the Lockheed factory in California had been taking up to three months by ship. Under the aegis of the Canadian Pacific Railway, the initial organisation was set up in Montreal in July 1940, and in November the first seven Hudsons made the crossing from Newfoundland to Northern Ireland.

Before April 1941, because of American neutrality, deliveries from California to the Canadian border had been made by civilians, but following the passage of the Lease-Lend Act it became possible for USAAF pilots to fly the aircraft direct to Montreal. This became the headquarters of the AFO, and Gander in Newfoundland and Prestwick in Scotland became the principal departure and arrival airfields. Hudsons were joined by Catalinas, Fortresses and Liberators on the direct crossing, and with the creation of a new base in Labrador it became possible to fly intermediate-range types in stages via Reykjavik, in Iceland. With American participation in the war, a further staging post was established in Greenland to enable fighters to be flown, rather than shipped, across the Atlantic. Subsequently, a second route was established for the delivery of aircraft to the Middle East, involving a journey via the Caribbean, Brazil and Ascension Island in the South Atlantic to the West African coast, and then across North Africa to Egypt.

In March 1943 Ferry Command became No 45 Group of the new Transport Command, whose other components were No 44 Group, dealing with transport based in Britain, No 216 in the Middle East and No 179 Wing in India. Subsequently, No 279 Group was formed in the Southeast Asia Command, and No 114 under Air Headquarters, West Africa. Meanwhile, another development was the formation of No 46 Group for the transport of airborne forces, for which No 38 Group of Fighter Command was also created.

The airborne forces groups used not only transport and heavy bomber types for carrying paratroops, but also gliders for guns and vehicles. The principal gliders were the American WACO Haig, known as the Hadrian in the RAF, which could accommodate up to 13 troops or light vehicles such as jeeps; the General Aircraft Hamilcar, designed to carry light tanks; and the Airspeed Horsa, with room for 26 troops or a variety of other loads such as jeeps, 25-pdr guns or parts for combat bridges. Towing aircraft used included Albemarles, Halifaxes, Stirlings and Dakotas.

The Dakota was also one of the principal general transport aircraft used by Transport Command, the RAF having no aircraft of this type at the start of the war apart from the obsolete bomber-transports of the 1930s. The first purpose-built British heavy transport aircraft was the Avro York, a development of the

Lancaster bomber with a completely new fuselage. The first Yorks became available in 1943, the third prototype being fitted out as a flying conference room for the personal use of the prime minister. In its normal configuration, with 24 passengers, the York had a range of 2700 miles (4345 km).

The airborne forces groups served in the landings in Sicily, in Normandy, at Arnhem and during the Rhine crossing in 1945. In the preliminary stages of the D-Day landings, more than 4000 paratroops were dropped, while nearly 500 arrived by glider with 17 guns, 44 jeeps and 55 motorcycles, as a result of the activities of Nos 38 and 46 Groups. For the Arnhem landing a total of 616 gliders were despatched in two waves, with 14 squadrons supplying the tow aircraft, while paratroops were dropped by American Dakotas. For the Rhine crossing a total of 440 gliders were used.

Left: Hudsons destined for Coastal Command await dispatch from the Lockheed plant in California. Hudsons were the first type to be flown, rather than shipped, to Britain

Below: WACO Hadrian troop-carrying gliders in a flooded field near Eindhoven in Holland

Another aspect of wartime transport was the clandestine operations carried out to drop and pick up agents in occupied Europe, and to supply arms, ammunition and other equipment to the resistance forces in France and elsewhere. The original unit carrying out these tasks in support of the resistance movement in France was No 138 Squadron, joined in February 1942 by No 161. Whitleys were the first type used for dropping agents and stores, often carrying bombs which were released over communications targets to disguise the true nature of their missions. As the war progressed, Havocs, Hudsons, Stirlings and Halifaxes also came into use, while for retrieving agents from occupied France the Lysander came into its own, its short take-off and landing ability making it eminently suitable for flying in and out of improvised landing strips in confined spaces.

AIRLIFTS AND EMERGENCIES, 1945-56

Above: The Avro York, a passenger development of the Lancaster bomber, which was used extensively during the Berlin airlift

Previous page: This Handley Page Hastings C.Mk 1A took part in the Allied airlift that broke the Soviet blockade of West Berlin

With the surrender of Japan in August 1945 and the end of the Second World War, transport became one of the RAF's main tasks. By the beginning of 1946 an average of 9000 passengers a month, mainly repatriated prisoners of war and replacements for staff at overseas bases, were being carried to and from the Far East. As well as Dakotas and Yorks, large numbers of converted Stirlings and Halifaxes were employed for these duties. Initially, transport versions of the heavy bombers simply had the gun positions faired over and carried baggage in the bomb bays, but special transport versions of both Stirling and Halifax were produced.

In January 1946 Transport Command's 42 squadrons and five flights were operating well over 1000 aircraft. In Britain three squadrons each of Stirlings and Yorks and another of Dakotas were operating internal routes, while one each of Dakotas and Warwicks covered European theatre communications. Four squadrons of Dakotas served in the Middle East, and 11 squadrons of Dakotas, supplemented by one each of Liberators and Douglas Skymasters, the military counterpart of the DC-4 civil airliner as the Dakota was of the DC-3, were based in India and Southeast Asia. In addition, six squadrons of Liberators, three of Dakotas and one of Yorks were engaged in trooping flights between India and the UK, while another squadron of Dakotas operated the Australia-Japan service. Six squadrons of Halifaxes were still assigned to airborne forces, three in the UK, two in the Middle East and one in Southeast Asia.

In common with other commands, however, Transport Command was to lose many of these units during the next year. However repatriation was not the only duty it was called on to perform. Sunderland squadrons based at Singapore were busy distributing food and medical supplies throughout the Far East during 1946, and within the next few years there was to be a great deal of movement as the British forces were withdrawn from the former outposts of the empire.

In 1947 India was partitioned to form the independent states of India and Pakistan, and the bulk of British forces were withdrawn, leaving behind only a limited number of advisers helping with the formation of new armed forces. The same year saw British control of Palestine, never particularly firm, become impossible, and from May 1948 the country was partitioned, again with an accompanying British withdrawal. Burma, too, became independent in 1949, and in February of that year there was an evacuation of women and children by a Sunderland of No 209 Squadron.

Nearer home, there was the problem of administering the defeated Axis states. In Italy, which had surrendered in 1943, but where fighting against the Germans had continued until May 1945, the principal problem was disposing of the stocks of explosives left behind by the various forces. Germany, however, presented a more complicated problem, being divided into four zones occupied by Soviet, American, British and French forces. The capital, Berlin, although inside the Soviet zone, was similarly divided.

The British Air Forces of Occupation consisted of No 2 Group, formerly of Bomber Command and the 2nd Tactical Air Force, along with some other elements of 2nd TAF, and their immediate task was disarming the Luftwaffe. This process, known as Operation Eclipse, involved processing nearly a million people, disposing of 5000 aircraft and destroying 220,000 tons (223,520,000 kg) of munitions and 195,000,000 rounds of ammunition. In March 1948, however, the Soviet administration began to restrict access by road to the non-Soviet zones of Berlin, and when road traffic was stopped completely in June, RAF and USAAF aircraft were pressed into service to supply the city by air.

The RAF contribution consisted of an eventual total of 40 Yorks, 40 Dakotas and 14 Handley Page Hastings transports. The last was a purpose-built military transport first flown in 1946; the first examples entered service in 1948, and along with later models served until 1968. Sunderland flying boats were also used in the early stages of the airlift, flying between the River Elbe and the Havel lake in Berlin, until the waters froze over. At the same time, a Combined Airlift Task Force was formed to co-ordinate British and American flights, and by the time the blockade was officially lifted in May 1949 the RAF had carried nearly 300,000 tons (304,800 tonnes) of supplies and nearly 70,000 passengers in just under 50,000 flights.

The De Havilland Vampire F.1, the second jet fighter to enter RAF service

As well as these demonstrations of its new capacity for large-scale transport operations over long distances, the RAF in the immediate post-war years was also returning to some familiar pre-war scenes in its old peace-keeping and anti-terrorist role. In Indonesia, liberated from Dutch rule by the Japanese and then from the Japanese invaders, three squadrons of Mosquitos and two of Thunderbolts from Singapore were involved in action against insurrections fomented by the Dutch.

In the following year a new series of operations, code-named Firedog, was started in support of army counter-terrorist operations in Malaya. Ironically, the terrorists were members of the resistance organisation trained and equipped by the British during the Japanese occupation who refused to surrender their arms in 1948 and started a guerrilla campaign using arms supplied by China. The ensuing state of emergency was not finally lifted until 1960, and in the intervening 10 years the campaign was to see some interesting innovations.

Initially, the RAF's contribution consisted mainly of ground attacks by Mosquitos, Beaufighters, Ansons and Sunderlands, supported by Dakota transports. Photo-reconnaissance Spitfires and Mosquitos also photographed large areas of the peninsula until replaced by Meteor FR.10s, the PR version of the Meteor F.8 fighter-bomber, in November 1953. Another jet fighter-bomber to serve in Malaya was the de Havilland Vampire in its FB.5 and FB.9 versions. The Vampire was the RAF's second jet fighter: it entered service with Fighter Command in March 1946, and was armed, like the Meteor, with four 20-mm cannon. By 1950 Vampires were in service with five regular and one Auxiliary Air Force squadron in the UK, as well as equipping all four fighter squadrons in Germany, where the BAFO had reverted to its earlier title of 2nd Tactical Air Force. In the Middle East another five squadrons were equipped with Vampires.

Although jet powered, the Vampire was not a sophisticated aircraft by contemporary standards, having no radar or power-operated controls, and its main use was as a two-seat trainer. The first two-seat version was a private venture night fighter with radar. This model was ordered by Egypt, but taken over by the RAF after an embargo on arms exports to Egypt, and served as the NF.10 until replaced by De Havilland Venoms and night fighter versions of the Meteor. The Venom was based on the Vampire, using the same twin-boom tail layout but with a 4850-lb (2200-kg) static thrust De Havilland Ghost engine in place of the much less powerful Goblin. This resulted in maximum speed being raised from around 550 mph (885 km/h) for the Vampire to 640 mph (1030 km/h).

Among the new piston-engined aircraft to serve in Malaya was one type specifically designed for the

Far left: The Handley Page Hastings served with Transport Command for 20 years until 1968. This is one of a small number retained for signals work, photographed in July 1976

Left: Prototype of the Vickers Valetta transport, which entered service in 1948

De Havilland Hornet F.3. Originally designed for service in the Far East, the Hornet was the RAF's fastest piston-engined fighter

Far East. The De Havilland Hornet, derived from the Mosquito, was powered by two 2030-hp Merlins and with a maximum speed of 472 mph (760 km/h) was the fastest piston-engined aircraft to serve with the RAF. Using drop tanks the Hornet had a range of 2500 miles (4023 km), but its arrival was overshadowed by that of the new, and even faster, jet fighters, and only four home-based Fighter Command squadrons used it. Following its withdrawal from service in 1950, however, the F.3 fighter-bomber models, which could carry two 1000-lb (454-kg) bombs in addition to the standard armament of four 20-mm cannon, were shipped to the Far East, where they equipped three squadrons.

Serving alongside the Hornet in the ground-attack role in the early 1950s was the Bristol Brigand. The Brigand was originally built as a torpedo bomber replacement for the Bristol Beaufighter, and was designed to carry two torpedoes and a three-man crew. The first few produced were delivered to Coastal Command in this form, but it was then decided to adapt the type as a light bomber. With four 20-mm cannon and able to carry 2000-lb (907-kg) of bombs or rockets under the wings, it entered service in the Middle East in 1949, three years after its abortive start with Coastal Command.

The replacement for the Lancaster heavy bomber was another Avro design, the Lincoln. The Lincoln's original designation was Lancaster Mk IV, but it was a bigger, more powerful aircraft than its predecessor, able to fly at a much higher altitude and armed with twin 0.5-in Brownings in nose, tail and dorsal turrets. A large production programme was planned, but the first production examples did not appear until April 1945, and orders were reduced in consequence. There was little call for strategic bombing in the Malayan campaign, but a remarkable achievement of the type was the dropping of 200,000,000 leaflets over 200 separate terrorist positions in a single day in October 1953. This operation was carried out by one RAF and one RAAF squadron, both using Lincolns: the leaflets offered the guerrillas rewards if they surrendered.

Another method of broadcasting propaganda was the use of aircraft equipped with powerful loudspeakers to address the guerrillas directly. The first experiments were made with army co-operation Austers in November 1952, and the following year 2000-watt speakers were installed in Dakotas. These could be heard up to 2500 yards (2286 m) away from a Dakota flying at 2500 ft (762 m), so that by flying at just above stalling speed in a box pattern the messages could be rendered audible for continuous periods of 30 seconds.

In the early 1950s the Dakotas were replaced by the Vickers Valetta, a twin-engined transport based on the Viking commercial airliner. The Valetta could carry 36 people over a range of 290 miles (467 km), or two and a half tons (2540 kg) of freight 1600 miles (2575 km), and its main task was supply-dropping to ground forces.

For casualty evacuation in the Malayan jungle, helicopters were introduced in 1950 in the form of the Westland Dragonfly, a licence-built version of the

Right: The Westland Whirlwind, based on the Sikorsky S-55, was introduced by No 155 Squadron in September 1954

American Sikorsky S-51. The Dragonfly could carry a pair of stretchers in special panniers, one on each side of the fuselage. This was rather a meagre payload, and considerably greater capacity was provided by the Westland Whirlwind, based on the Sikorsky S-55, which was first operated in Malaya by a Royal Navy squadron, before No 155 Squadron was formed with the type in September 1954. The Whirlwinds were used not only for cas-evac work, but also as troop carriers, and could carry up to 10 passengers or six stretcher cases.

One of the few British-designed helicopters to serve with the RAF, the Bristol Sycamore, also appeared in Malaya in 1954. Earlier deliveries had been made to Coastal Command for rescue work, and the Sycamore had half the carrying capacity of the Whirlwind. In this respect it had few advantages over the Scottish Aviation Pioneer, which could fly with an airspeed as low as 36 mph (58 km/h) and could carry five passengers, or four soldiers with their equipment, or a stretcher case and attendant. Its short take-off and landing performance was also useful, and throughout 1955 the first six to arrive flew an average of well over two sorties a day.

Malaya was not the only area where the RAF was called on to suppress rebellion. In Kenya the activities of the mysterious Mau Mau organisation resulted in the proclamation of a state of emergency in 1952, and this remained in force until 1959. In the early stages of the anti-Mau Mau operations, Harvards were used to bomb suspected hideouts after being detached from training schools in Rhodesia and fitted with racks for 19-lb (8.6-kg) bombs. At the other end of the scale Lincolns were used to demonstrate the effects of 500-lb

Left: Loading a jeep through the cargo doors of a Valetta

Below: Iraqi air force De Havilland Venom FB.50, export version of the RAF's FB.1

A Hunting Percival Provost trainer and its Jet Provost successor

Right: A Bristol Brigand equipped for crew training with nose radome and blacked-out rear cockpit

Far right: Gloster Meteor T.7 trainers

Hunting Percival
JET PROVOST

RH798

(227-kg) and 1000-lb (454-kg) bombs, though with little chance of hitting anyone that could hear them coming.

By the time of the Kenyan operations, the RAF was also involved in the Korean war, where the remarkable strides made by military aviation in the few years since the end of the Second World War were clearly demonstrated. While Sunderlands carried out coastal patrols and air-sea rescue missions, the first jet fighter combat was developing in the skies over Korea, as American F-86 Sabres fought North Korean MiG-15s. One result of the conflict in Korea, and the associated intensification of the Cold War, was an abrupt reversal of the rundown in RAF strength, with the number of aircraft in service being raised from 4510

English Electric Canberra T.17, electronic countermeasures training variant of the RAF's first jet bomber

Inset: A Canberra B.2 of No 57 Squadron in the mid-1950s

in 1950 to the post-war peak of 6338 in 1952, while the number of personnel in the service rose less dramatically to 277,000.

In the matter of equipment, a doubling of the rate of aircraft production was planned, with particular emphasis on the new English Electric Canberra. The twin-jet Canberra was the RAF's first jet-propelled bomber, and a major setback was the failure of the radar bombing system which had been specified. However, the Canberra's basic performance was such that the contemporary fighters were too slow to intercept it, and its introduction into service in 1951 was the start of a career that was to last well into the 1980s.

The original Canberra carried a typical bomb load of six 1000-lb (454-kg) bombs in an internal bay, but subsequent armament options included a gun pack mounting four 20-mm cannon under the fuselage and additional wing pylons for bombs or rocket pods. It was also built in photographic reconnaissance versions, and converted to produce electronic warfare, training and target models, as well as forming the basis for the Martin B-57 Night Intruder built in the United States for the USAF. By 1955 Canberras equipped 24 of the 31 Bomber Command squadrons based in Britain, and all four of the bomber squadrons with the 2nd TAF in Germany.

While the Canberra was under development, eight Lincoln squadrons were equipped with Boeing B-29 Superfortresses, which received the RAF name Washington. These were supplied under the Mutual

Defence Assistance Programme following the creation of the North Atlantic Treaty Organisation in 1949. Other aircraft supplied by the United States under the MDAP included four squadrons of Lockheed Neptune maritime patrol aircraft for Coastal Command in 1952. By this time flying boats, with their limited range and payload, had become outmoded: their great virtue of being able to operate without prepared airstrips had been nullified by the huge numbers of airfields constructed during the war.

Perhaps the most significant of the American imports in the early 1950s was the North American F-86 Sabre, built in Canada for the RAF. Experience in Korea with Meteors flown by Royal Australian Air Force squadrons showed that the British fighter was markedly inferior to the MiG-15, and with no successor to the Meteor in immediate prospect, Sabres were used to equip 10 fighter squadrons with the 2nd TAF in Germany and two Fighter Command units from 1952.

The first new British fighter to succeed the Meteor, Vampire and Venom was the Supermarine Swift. Despite setting a new world speed record of just under 738 mph (1188 km/h) in September 1953 the Swift was not a success. It equipped only one fighter squadron, though another two squadrons in Germany used photo-reconnaissance versions. In any case, the Swift had been ordered in the first place as insurance against the failure of another new type, which in the event turned out to be one of the most successful of all jet fighter designs.

The Hawker Hunter entered service with Fighter Command in July 1954, and by 1958 all RAF day fighter squadrons in Europe were flying the F.6 version. Widely regarded as the best subsonic jet fighter ever built, the Hunter combined a top speed of 715 mph (1151 km/h) at sea level with the ability to climb to 45,000 ft (13,716 m) in just over seven minutes and a range in excess of 1800 miles (2897 km). Armament was four 30-mm Aden cannon, an overdue improvement on the early post-war standard of four 20-mm Hispanos, and for ground attacks the F.6 could carry two 1000-lb (454-kg) bombs or alternative weapons under the wings. The Hunter was also beautiful, and its exceptional manoeuvrability enabled the all-black examples used by No 111 Squadron as the Black Arrow to become the world's best aerobatic display team in the late 1950s.

Following the Hunter into service in 1956, the Gloster Javelin was the first purpose-built night fighter and all-weather interceptor provided for the RAF, and by 1960 it equipped 10 home-based fighter squadrons and another three in Germany. The original AI.10 radar was later replaced by the American APQ-43, and in 1958 the FAW.7 introduced Firestreak infra-red homing air-to-air missiles, the

Right: Trials of flight refuelling equipment for Valiant tankers: a Gloster Javelin takes fuel from a Canberra B.2

Below: Hawker Hunter F.6 of No 234 Operational Conversion Unit in April 1974

31
XG196

original gun armament of four Adens being reduced to two on this model. Performance was no more than moderate, with a maximum speed of 680 mph (1094 km/h), but the Javelin was well equipped and popular with its pilots.

In the same year as the Javelin entered service the RAF received its first jet transport aircraft in the shape of the De Havilland Comet C.2, a military development of the Comet I civil airliner offering the useful combination of accommodation for 44 passengers and a range of 2500 miles (4023 km). An electronics version was also built as the E.2.

Meanwhile, the development of a British nuclear bomb, the first test of which was carried out off north-western Australia in October 1952, had been accompanied by the issue of specifications for new bombers designed to carry the weapon. While the more advanced Victor and Vulcan were being developed by Handley Page and Avro, the Vickers Valiant was ordered as an interim carrier for the weapon, and the first production Valiant was delivered to the RAF in January 1955, entering squadron service later that year. The first operational atomic bomb was dropped by a Valiant on 11 October 1956: later the same month other Valiants were dropping conventional bombs in the opening round of Operation Musketeer, the ill-conceived Anglo-French-Israeli invasion of Egypt.

The nationalisation of the Suez Canal Company was the culmination of 10 years of growing Arab nationalism, that had involved the RAF in operations

in Aden and seen its withdrawal from some of its oldest bases in the Canal Zone. Apart from the French and Israeli units, amounting to 10 squadrons, and the carrier-borne units, an impressive RAF force was assembled for Musketeer. On Malta there were six squadrons of Canberras, four of Valiants and one of Shackletons, the maritime reconnaissance development of the Lincoln used by Coastal Command. On Cyprus there were another nine squadrons of Canberras, three each of Hastings and Valetta transports, four of Venom fighter-bombers, two of Hunters and one of Meteor night fighters, as well as another of photo-reconnaissance Valiants.

The campaign did not last long. On the night of 30 October and again the following morning Valiants bombed the Egyptian airfields, their attacks being followed up on the following four days by RAF and Fleet Air Arm fighter-bombers. On 5 November troops were landed by transport aircraft and by helicopter from the aircraft carriers and by midnight on 6 November international pressure had resulted in a cease-fire. On 22 December the last British and French troops left the occupied zone.

The Gloster Javelin all-weather fighter in its original configuration with four cannon in the wings

THE NUCLEAR DETERRENT AND THE V-FORCE

Previous page: A Vulcan B2 bomber armed with a Blue Steel nuclear missile. The missile had a range of 200 miles (320 km) allowing the aircraft to release the weapon from a stand-off position

During 1957 the Conservative government undertook a complete transformation of British defence policy. Published in April of that year, the Defence White Paper revealed the outlines of a new strategic concept based on the deterrent effect of a fresh generation of nuclear weapons. Since it was thought impossible for manned interceptor fighters to provide total protection against nuclear-armed enemy bombers, and since the result of even a very small number of such bombers penetrating British airspace were deemed totally unacceptable, it was decided that a smaller number of fighters should be committed to defence of the bomber bases, which according to the deterrent theory comprised the main defence of the UK. The White Paper also predicted that this defence would ultimately be vested in ballistic missiles: in the meantime it was the task of the RAF to maintain the V-bomber force and to ensure its survival in the opening phases of any war. In the longer term, defence of the relevant air bases would also be taken over by missiles, in this instance of the surface-to-air variety.

By this time the second and third of the new V-bombers were entering service. The Avro Vulcan was a large delta-winged machine of unorthodox configuration but wholly conventional construction, and as an alternative to its nuclear weapon load could carry 21 1000-lb (454-kg) conventional bombs, the same load as the first of the V-bombers, the Vickers Valiant. The Handley Page Victor, on the other hand, was a more conventional yet also more advanced type in terms of its aerodynamics, with conventionally configured but

Below: The first of the V-bombers to enter service was the Vickers Valiant. It saw service against Egyptian targets during the Suez Crisis, and tested all the British air-dropped nuclear weapons

With its crescent-shaped flying surfaces, the Handley Page Victor V-bomber was designed to operate at high altitude while maintaining a high-speed cruise at high subsonic speed. It was the last of the V-Bomber force

crescent-shaped flying surfaces to provide the required high-speed cruise at high subsonic speed at high altitude. Like the Vulcan, the Victor had the primary task of carrying a 10,000-lb (4536-kg) nuclear weapon over a range of 4000 miles (6440 km), but its bomb was large enough to allow the alternative accommodation of no fewer than 35 1000-lb (454-kg) 'iron' bombs in the conventional bombing role.

The first Vulcan squadron was No 83, which formed at RAF Waddington in May 1957. The second was No 101, previously an English Electric Canberra unit, which became operational at RAF Finningley during October, and the third squadron was No 617 that re-formed at RAF Scampton in May 1958. The Victor became operational during 1958, the first two units being Nos 10 and 15 Squadrons that formed at RAF Cottesmore in April and October of that Year. By the end of 1958, RAF Bomber Command mustered no less than 14 V-bomber squadrons including at Finningley No 18 Squadron, the command's specialised electronic countermeasures unit with Valiant and Canberra aircraft. The force comprised, in addition to the six squadrons listed above, eight Valiant B.1 squadrons deployed at RAF Wittering (Nos 49 and 138 Squadrons), RAF Marham (Nos 148, 207 and 214 Squadrons) and RAF Honington (Nos 7 and 90 Squadrons).

The primary weapon of the V-bomber force during the late 1950s was the free fall nuclear bomb code-named 'Blue Danube'. This had been developed at the Atomic Weapons Research and Development Establishment at Aldermaston and first exploded in an atypical fashion, during October 1952, off the Monte Bello islands in the Indian Ocean aboard the surplus frigate HMS *Plym*. The first operational bomb was delivered during November 1953 after a period of intense preparation undertaken at the RAF Bomber Command Armament School at Wittering, where training manuals and training courses were prepared, high security bomb shelters designed, and servicing and security procedures devised.

In concert with these preparations the RAF had been undertaking the upgrade of ten air bases to so-called 'Class One' condition suitable for V-bomber operations. These bases were RAF Coningsby, Cottesmore, Finningley, Gaydon, Honington, Marham, Scampton, Waddington, Wittering and Wyton: each was given a 10,000-ft (3050-m) runway including a 1000-ft (305-m) overrun, and these runways were each 200ft (61 m) wide and able to accept a 200,000-lb (90,720-kg) aeroplane. At each base there were taxiways and hardstandings for at least 16 aircraft, together with other essentials such as lighting, landing aids, upgraded air-traffic control equipment, storage and pipelines for the vast quantities of fuel required, and all the normal aircraft and weapons facilities for storage and maintenance.

With the aircraft and their essential infrastructure available, the task facing Bomber Command was to turn the V-bomber force into an effective weapon against the possibility of Soviet aggression. The primary task was deterrence, and this would only work if the anticipated enemy remained convinced that the V-bombers could survive any initial aggression and then use their high levels of serviceability and operational capability to penetrate Soviet airspace and drop their weapons on key targets. Such serviceability and operational capabilities could be ensured only by constant practice, and a measure of operational training under realistic conditions was provided by overseas deployments to areas of high tension, and indeed by real though conventional operations such as the Valiant attacks against Egyptian targets during the 1956 Suez operations.

During the early 1960s the capabilities of the V-bomber forces were improved steadily as all levels of personnel learned their tasks to perfection, as the aircraft and their ground facilities matured, and as the RAF devised methods of improving its deterrent theory. In this last aspect an important development was the dispersal system, in which the vulnerability of the V-bombers to a first strike was reduced by temporary and unscheduled deployment to alternative RAF air bases in times of heightened tension. Over the same period readiness procedures were improved, greater co-operation with the US Air Force was secured (including co-ordination of targeting plans) and the British 'Yellow Sun' thermonuclear free-fall bomb was introduced.

The dispersal programme allowed for the deployment of the V-bombers from their ten main bases to any of the large number of Bomber, Coastal, Fighter, Flying Training and Transport Command bases in the UK able to handle these aircraft, as well as to Royal Navy and Ministry of Aviation airfields. Practice dispersals became a standard part of the V-bomber training schedule. Tied into this concept was the readiness condition of the V-bomber force. This was based on the two levels of warning fixed in 1957. The strategic warning gave 24 hours' notice and demanded that 20 per cent of the V-bomber force should be at

Left: A 543 Squadron crew are scrambled at RAF Wyton in 1958. The record time from scramble to take-off of the Valiant was clocked at 6 minutes 59 seconds

High above the clouds flies a Handley Page Victor armed with a Blue Steel stand-off missile. The missile was designed and built by Avro and was in service with the RAF from 1964 until 1975

readiness within 2 hours, 40 per cent in 4 hours, 60 per cent in 8 hours, and 75 per cent within 24 hours. The tactical warning demanded that aircraft be at 15 minutes' readiness for 7 days or at 40 minutes' readiness for 30 days. It was all an expensive business, for additional air and ground crews were required for the 18-hour working day two shifts.

In 1962, and prepared with the 1963 opening of the Fylingdales early warning station in mind, RAF Bomber Command adopted the quick-reaction alert (QRA) procedure, in which each V-bomber squadron was required to maintain one aeroplane at 15-minute readiness. This reaction time was steadily cut as the RAF appreciated the growing threat posed by Soviet ballistic missiles targeted on British bases. Despite the 15 minutes demanded in the QRA procedure, V-bomber squadrons kept their QRA aircraft at about 4-minute readiness, and by the early 1960s this had been reduced to about 2-minute readiness, so that a warning from Fylingdales would allow all QRA aircraft to clear the anticipated detonation of any Soviet nuclear missile targeted on a British air base.

The principal weapon of the two more advanced V-bombers was to be neither nuclear or conventional free-fall bombs, however, but rather the Avro Blue Steel missile. This weapon entered development in 1954 as a stand-off nuclear missile powered by rocket using high-test peroxide and kerosene as its two liquid fuels: released at an altitude of between 35,000 and 40,000 ft (10,670 and 12,190 m), the Blue Steel was controlled by its onboard autopilot and inertial navigation system for a climb to higher altitude and then a steep dive towards the target at a range of more than 200 miles (322 km). The use of such a missile meant that the bomber did not have to overfly a heavily defended target area, and that it could in any event undertake evasive manoeuvres as soon as the missile had been launched.

By the end of 1960 Bomber Command's British main bases accommodated 18 operational squadrons: seven with the Valiant, four each with the Vulcan and Victor, and the last three with the Canberra. By the end of 1962 the figure was 15 nuclear-deterrent force squadrons: the Vulcan units were Nos 27, 83, and 617 Squadrons with the B.1 at Scampton. Nos 44, 50 and 101 Squadrons with the B.1A at Waddington, and Nos 9, 12 and 35 Squadrons with the B.2 at Coningsby; the Victor units were Nos 10 and 15 Squadrons with the B.1 at Cottesmore, Nos 100 and 139 Squadrons with the B.1 at Wittering, and Nos 55 and 57 with the B.1A at Honington.

Numbers may have been adequate but weapons were certainly not, because it was 1964 before the much delayed Blue Steel began to enter service. And by this date the operational requirement on which the V-bombers and the Blue Steel had been designed was undergoing a major and belated change. Speed and altitude were no longer adequate protection for bombers: the destruction of Gary Powers's Lockheed U-2 by a SAM over the USSR in 1962 had provided firm evidence of this fact. As a result the bombers were required to operate at increasingly low altitude at much reduced speed, and the Blue Steel was adapted for launch at heights of less than 1000 ft (305 m). It was appreciated even at this early stage that the range of the Blue Steel was hardly adequate for its planned strategic role, and ultimately the type was deployed on only 36 V-bombers: 24 Vulcan B.2s of Nos 23, 87 and 617 Squadrons at Scampton, and 12 Victor B.2s of Nos 100 and 139 Squadrons at Wittering.

Above: The RAF operated the Blue Steel missile from both the Vulcan and Victor. It was capable of speeds up to Mach 2 delivering a one-megaton thermonuclear warhead

But operations at low altitude place an entirely different set of aerodynamic and, more importantly, structural imperatives on aircraft, particularly as low-level turbulence imposes stresses for which the air-frames of the V-bombers were never designed. So the bombers themselves had to be modified and adapted to the new operating regime of low-level penetration. A low-altitude version of the Valiant was designed and built for flight trials as early as 1953, but no production orders had been placed. By 1964 even a small number of low-altitude hours was beginning to have its effect on the Valiant fleet, and the original Valiant B.1s were starting to show the strain in the form of cracked wing spars. Rather than embark on an expensive programme of rebuilding and structural strengthening of this obsolescent type, the RAF ordered the whole force to be scrapped. The Valiant had already been replaced in the QRA strategic force by the Vulcan and Victor, so that while three squadrons were still in service on the low-altitude tactical bombing role with the RAF's NATO forces in West Germany, two had already been phased into service as tankers.

Left: A Vickers Valiant tanker refuels a Valiant bomber. The requirement for the V-bombers to operate at low altitude eventually led to the scrapping of the Valiant force

The Vulcan and Victor were progressively upgraded and modified to suit them to the changing conditions in which they would have to operate. The B.1A conversions of the original Vulcan and Victor B.1 bombers provided significantly improved electronic countermeasures in the early 1960s, and were adapted for the carriage of the 'Yellow Sun Mk 2' free-fall thermonuclear weapon. a lightened version of the original 'Yellow Sun' fitted with the 'Red Snow' warhead, an improved type designed with the help of renewed American technical aid after the lifting of the nuclear freeze between the two countries imposed by the US Congress in 1946. More powerful engines were used in the new-built Victor and Vulcan B.2 bombers designed specifically for the carriage of the Blue Steel missile and the parachute-retarded 'lay-down' nuclear bomb being designed for use by the Royal Navy's Blackburn Buccaneer strike aircraft: this later matured as the WE 177. Just as important as the additional power of the new engines, moreover, was the fact that they were of the turbofan rather than turbojet variety as used in the B.1/1A aircraft: these more advanced

Above: A Handley Page Victor K.1A trails its three refuelling drogues. The RAF had realised the need for air-to-air refuelling to provide extra range and support to both its bomber and fighter forces and the Victor provided an excellent tanker aircraft

Right: A Vulcan B.2 with its low level camouflage comes into land during the late 1960s. The change in strategic bombing strategy from high level to low-level bombing was completed in 1966

Above: A Blue Steel stand-off nuclear missile about to be loaded aboard a Handley Page Victor B.2

Right: The unmistakable shape of an Avro Vulcan B.2 strategic bomber

Below: An Avro Vulcan with its distinct delta wing flying over the English countryside

A Vulcan B.2 makes a low pass with its undercarriage down and its bomb bay doors open. This aircraft was able to carry up to 21,000 lb in the internal bomb bay

engines offered far more economical operation, helping to offset the considerable reduction in range imposed by low-level operations.

By the end of 1965 the 13 home-based squadrons of RAF Bomber Command comprised nine Vulcan and four Victor units: the Vulcan force was made up of six Vulcan B.1/1A and three Vulcan B.2 units, while the Victor force had one Victor B.1A and two Victor B.2

units, the last squadron having Victor B(K).1As in the combined bomber and in-flight refuelling roles.

In the next year the first Victor squadron switched to the K.1 tanker, a specialised conversion with provision for three-point in-flight refuelling. Another two squadrons, including one re-formed unit, were subsequently equipped with tanker conversions. This marked a late realisation by the RAF of the value, indeed necessity, of such aircraft to provide greater range and to provide damaged aircraft with the fuel that might bring them home. Another conversion of the Victor was the SR.2 strategic reconnaissance platform with cameras and other sensors in the erstwhile bomb bay. This equipped one squadron from 1965, and was used mainly for long-range oceanic reconnaissance.

In mid-1966 the Vulcan force, which during the previous 12 years had been kept at a state of constant readiness to deliver nuclear weapons, was switched to the low-level penetration role with special terrain-following radar. The conversion to the low-level role was completed in 1966, and RAF bomber Command's V-bomber force at that time comprised Nos 44, 50 and 101 Squadrons at Waddington with Vulcan B.1s (being replaced by B.2s) and 'Yellow Sun MK 2' Bombs, Nos 9, 12 and 35 Squadrons at Cottesmore with Vulcan B.2s and WE 177 bombs, Nos 27, 83 and 617 Squadrons at Scampton with Vulcan B.2s and Blue Steel missiles, and Nos 100 and 139 Squadrons at Wittering with Victor B.2s and Blue Steel missiles. The Blue Steel procedure was a low-level approach to the target before a sharp climb to 12,000 ft (3660 m), release of the missile and a swift reversal of course before a dive 'onto the deck' for the return to base.

In line with the 1957 Defence White Paper, the RAF had also begun to develop a ballistic missile arm to complement and then supposedly to supplant the V-bomber force. The British had no suitable missile of their own, so while such a weapon was being developed, under the terms of a February 1958 agreement the US Air Force loaned the RAF 60 Thor intermediate-range ballistic missiles. These each carried a megaton-class warhead, and with a range of 1500 miles (2415 km) could reach deep into the western USSR from British bases. The missiles were deployed at RAF bases with RAF crews, but the warheads were kept under American control for use only after joint agreement by both countries. The missiles were allocated to 20 squadrons at dispersed bases in East Anglia, Lincolnshire and Yorkshire, each squadron having five launch crews.

A high level of proficiency was reached in test firings at Vandenberg Air Force Base in California. But by the early 1960s the USA was concentrating its efforts on intercontinental ballistic missiles able to strike at the USSR from the continental USA, and it was announced that from 1964 logistic support for the Thors would be ended. The British were already aware of the limitations of the Thor system: the type was based above ground and could not be launched in under 15 minutes, and was therefore hopelessly vulnerable to a Soviet first strike. In 1963, therefore, all the missiles were returned to the USA. The RAF was to have replaced its Thors with a British missile, the Blue Streak. This originated from a 1955 requirement for a medium-range ballistic missile able to deliver a megaton-class warhead over 2000 miles (3220 km) after launch from an underground (and therefore comparatively invulnerable) site. The programme was beset by a number of technical problems, but the missile was in itself promising in its original role and as a possible space launcher. The Blue Streak was to be used in parallel with an updated Blue Steel Mk2 offering 1000-mile (620-km) range, but in the early 1960s both programmes were cancelled because of the apparent economic as well as military advantages of ordering a promising American missile, the air-launched Douglas Skybolt that could be carried by the B.2 versions of the Vulcan and Victor.

The US government then cancelled the Skybolt, and the RAF was left with no viable nuclear deterrent beyond the few years left to the current combination of V-bombers armed with the Blue Steel Mk 1 missile plus 'Yellow Sun Mk 2' and WE 177 nuclear bombs. The switch to low-level operations enhanced the viability of the combination in its last years, but the death knell of the RAF's nuclear deterrent was sealed with the US government's offer of the submarine-launched Polaris missile as an alternative to the Skybolt. This offer was gratefully received by an embarrassed British government, and from 1968 the nuclear deterrent role was increasingly taken over by the Royal Navy's new 'Resolution' class missile-launching submarines. Inevitably the V-bomber forces was contracted and switched to other tasks. No 12 Squadron was disbanded in December 1967, followed in September and December 1968 by Nos 100 and 139 Squadrons, and in August 1969 by No 83 Squadron. In the same year Nos 9 and 35 Squadrons became part of the Near East Air Force Strike Wing at RAF Akrotiri in Cyprus. Between 1968 and 1970 the Blue Steel was retired, its two operating squadrons (Nos 27 and 617 Squadrons) being switched to free-fall bombing and maritime reconnaissance, and the QRA was formally ended in June 1969. Just as decisively, one year earlier Bomber Command had ceased to exist, becoming instead No 1 Group within the Strike Command organisation created to combine and supersede RAF Bomber and Fighter Commands. The Victors were successively converted to the strategic reconnaissance and tanker roles, and by the mid-1970s the V-bomber force had shrunk to six Vulcans B.2 units (Nos 9, 35, 44, 50, 101, and 617 Squadrons) operating in the free-fall bomber role with conventional and/or nuclear weapons as part of the UK's air commitment to NATO tactical assets. The last Vulcans were retired in 1982 after a small but important role in the war against Argentina, in which the aircraft undertook the longest bombing raids ever flown, conventional attacks from Ascension Island against Stanley Airport and radar installations in the Falklands with the aid of Victor tankers.

Right: A test launch of a Thor, the missile which served briefly with the RAF in the late 1950s and early 1960s

ARPA

THE MISSILE'S FALSE DAWN

The notorious 1957 Defence White Paper was based, among other things, on the notion that the day of the manned warplane was virtually over, and that within the foreseeable future the missile would reign supreme in the skies. That this premise was patently wrong is easy to see now, and even at the time attracted a large volume of adverse criticism. Yet at the time when technology of all types was advancing by leaps and bounds, there was a certain logic to the concept of the White Paper's authors: where they went wrong was in accepting a particular technological premise without any regard for other possibilities derived from equally valid technological reasoning. Be that as it may, the White Paper envisaged a man-less sky, and for political purposes exacerbated by economic considerations such a concept was imposed on an unwilling RAF.

The first fruit of the concept was a scaling-down of RAF Fighter Command's already meagre fighter resources and, in virtually equal measure, the scaling-up of surface-to-air missile defences. Given the fact that the defence of the UK was deemed to rest on the deterrent capability of the V-bomber force in face of a potential enemy as large as the USSR, conventional fighter protection of the country along the lines of the Second World War national defence was thought not only impossible but also needless. The crux of the matter was defence of the V-bomber bases by a small but highly capable force of manned interceptors, initially equipped with the obsolescent Hawker Hunter cannon-armed subsonic fighter and then with the new generation of English Electric Lightning missile-armed supersonic fighters. It was expected, though, that defence of the bomber bases and thus of the UK would ultimately rest with surface-to-air missiles.

In December 1958 Fighter Command declared operational its first Bristol Bloodhound surface-to-air missile squadron. Such was the priority allocated to this all-important type that two years later there were 12 Bloodhound squadrons. The missile had a proximity-fused HE warhead, Mach 2 speed and considerable range, the last provided by the use of two liquid-propellant ramjet sustainers that took over after the four solid-propellant rocket boosters had dropped away. Accurate homing was generated by semi-active radar guidance, in which the missile homed on the electro-magnetic radiation reflected by the target after being illuminated by the missile's fire-control radar. Some 352 Bloodhounds were operated by four three-

Previous page: An English Electric Lightning F.1 armed with Red Top missiles shows off its clean lines

Right: A Bristol Bloodhound surface-to-air missile is fired during tests. The government and senior officers during the late 1950s considered that the age of the aircraft was over and that the only way forward would be with missiles for both defensive and offensive missions

squadron missile wings each centred on a tactical control centre: No 2 Wing at RAF Lindholme protected the northern complex of V-bomber bases, No 24 Wing at RAF Watton protected the East Anglian V-bomber bases, No 148 Wing at RAF North Coates protected RAF Coningsby, Scampton and Waddington plus the Thor complex at RAF Hemswell, and No 151 Wing at RAF North Luffenham protected the southern complex of V-bomber bases.

It soon became clear, however, that the surface-to-air missile was in itself a limited weapon, and in combination with a round of defence cuts forced on the service by the government this meant that by the end of 1964 the Bloodhound squadrons had declined in number to three, though each of these fielded the much improved Bloodhound Mk 2 missile able to engage low-altitude targets. The missile and its fire-control radar were also air-transportable, meaning that the service could deploy these limited assets where most needed.

Manned interceptors were still required, therefore, and in July 1960 the Lightning F.1 began to enter squadron service as replacement for the Hunter in the interceptor role, freeing the Hunters for conversion into fighter-bombers or, as they were now termed, ground-attack aircraft. The Lightning finally left British service in 1988, a creditable record of longevity for an unusual but limited aeroplane. Derived from the P.1 supersonic research type with superimposed Rolls-Royce Avon turbojets and angular but highly swept flying surfaces, the Lightning possessed phenomenal acceleration and rate of climb, could reach Mach 2, and had a ceiling in the order of 60,000 ft (19,685 m). These were excellent attributes for an interceptor, but they went with typically British failings such as wholly inadequate range and particularly limited armament. Range was improved in variants up to the final Lightning F.6 by the enlargement of internal fuel capacity, the addition of a semi-permanent ventral tank, the installation of an in-flight refuelling probe, and provision for under- and over-wing drop tanks, while armament always remained inadequate. The F.1 had two 30-mm cannon, packs of unguided rockets (seldom fitted) and only two Firestreak heat-seeking air-to-air missiles, all used with the aid of Ferranti Airpass radar once the fighter had been vectored into the right area by the ground-control interception organisation. The internal cannon were deleted in the F.3, which adopted the more capable Red Top version of the Firestreak in compensation. The missile arma-

Twenty-five Lightnings and Hunters of 111 Squadron fly in a mass diamond formation

Lightning
T.4

H
XP750

ment was always the Lightning's most limited feature, for these early heat-seeking missiles were capable only of attack from the rear or, in the case of the Firestreak, the flank: hardly a suitable weapon for a fighter designed to intercept and attack head-on the bombers flying towards the UK with nuclear bombs. The Firestreak remained the Lightning's primary weapon right to the interceptor's demise, but later variants of the fighter reintroduced fixed cannon armament, in this instance a pair of 30-mm cannon in the forward section of the ventral tank.

As the Lightning began to enter service, RAF Fighter Command could muster 17 squadrons of fighters in the UK (ten of Gloster Javelin all-weather fighters and seven of Hunter clear-weather fighters), while the other 15 British fighter squadrons were located overseas: in Aden was a single Hunter squadron, in Kenya a single Hunter squadron, in Singapore single squadrons of de Havilland Venom fighter-bombers and Gloster Meteor night-fighters, and in West Germany three squadrons of Javelins and six squadrons of Hunters.

The defence cuts of the early 1960's resulted in a savage curtailment of these forces, and by 1965 there were only 19 fighter squadrons, a mere six of them belonging to Fighter Command with about 60 Lightnings and, in the short term, Javelins: this was the level maintained for home fighter defence for the next four years. In 1965 the other fighter assets comprised two squadrons of Hunter ground-attack fighters with RAF Transport Command, two squadrons of Javelins with the 2nd Allied Tactical Air Force (latterly RAF Germany), one squadron of Javelins on Cyprus with the Near East Air Force (latterly Middle East Air Force), three squadrons of Hunters with Aden Strike Wing, and with the Far East Air Force a squadron of Hunters in Hong Kong, a squadron of Hunters in Singapore and in the same place two squadrons of Javelins.

It is worth noting here that in recent years there had been several organisational and title changes affecting the RAF. In September 1957 the Army Air Corps had been created to absorb those RAF assets connected directly with the light support of the army in the field, in 1958 No 90 (Signals) Group became Signals Command, in 1960 No 38 Group was formed as a self-contained and air-transportable tactical unit within Transport Command, which in 1967 became Air Support Command. Other changes have been mentioned above, the most important being the amalgamation of Bomber and Fighter Commands as RAF Strike Command, Air Support Command later absorbed Training Command to become Support Command, and this created the organisation of the present RAF with two primary commands.

In any mention of RAF deployment in this period it is notable that with the exception of the nuclear and first-line interceptor forces the bulk of the RAF's strength was located outside the UK. A modest strength was maintained in Germany, but consider-

Previous page main picture: A Lightning F.3 of 111 Squadron is prepared for flight. The Lightning was designed as a pure local defence interceptor with a high speed climb able to operate at high altitude

Previous page inset left: Lightning F.6 interceptors of No 23 Squadron in formation

Previous page inset right: A Lightning T.4 two seater trainer

Above: De Havilland Firestreak air-to-air missiles on a late-model Javelin

Left: The Gloster Javelin was the first British designed night and all-weather fighter

Right: A Hunter ground attack aircraft of 65 Squadron is prepared for a mission. It was armed with four 30 mm Aden cannon and could carry up to 2000 lbs (900 kg) of ordnance

able assets were located on Cyprus, in Aden and in the Far East, all troublespots where the UK's declining interest in imperial ties demanded support as the relevant countries were shifted towards independence. Essential in this overseas commitment was RAF Transport Command, which needed long-range aircraft for strategic purposes, medium-range aircraft for operational purposes and short-range aircraft for purely tactical purposes. Several Second World War types and their descendants were still in service, but from the mid-1950s a new series of aircraft began to appear. First was the short/medium-range Blackburn Beverley, which reached squadron service in 1956. This large pod-and-boom type was powered by four piston engines with reversible-pitch propellers allowing the machine to land in as little as 225 yards (205 m). The deep fuselage could accommodate 94 troops, or 82 casualties or up to 45,000 lb (20,412 kg) of freight carried over a range of 230 miles (370 km), or alternatively a 29,000-lb (13,154-kg) payload carried over 1300 miles (2090 km).

Longer-range capability, without any pretence at STOL performance or airdropping capability, was the strength of the Bristol Britannia that began to enter service in 1959. This was powered by four turboprops, and could carry 125 troops over transcontinental ranges. The year 1961 saw the advent of the Armstrong Whitworth Argosy, another four-turboprop type, but in this instance of pod and twin-boom type for the short/medium-range role, with 60 troops, or 54 paratroops or 48 casualties. In 1962 the Comet C.4 arrived for the movement of up to 94 passengers (compared with the Comet C.2's 44 passengers) on the power of four turbojets.

262
291

ROYAL AIR FORCE TRANSPORT COMMAND
A

Top left: Pod-and-boom Blackburn Beverleys at Changi Airport in 1967

Bottom left: British Paras jump from an Armstrong Whitworth Argosy. The Argosy was capable of carrying 54 paratroops

Bottom middle: The Argosy was designed to operate in the short/medium airlift role and first flew in 1959

Top right: The Comet 4 entered service with the RAF in 1962 and enabled 94 passengers to be carried far more quickly than any other service aircraft available at the time

Bottom right: A head-on shot of an Argosy high above the clouds as it flies in formation during a large-scale parachute exercise

Above: A Vickers VC-10 of Transport Command

Right: The Westland (Bristol) Belvedere was an all-British design. It provided the support of the Army in battlefield conditions. The RAF has always been tasked with the medium and heavy helicopter support of the Army

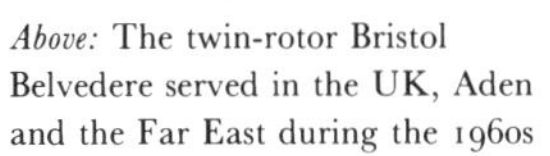
Above: The twin-rotor Bristol Belvedere served in the UK, Aden and the Far East during the 1960s

More capable still was the BAC VC10 C.1 that reached service in 1966. Like the Comet this was a simple adaptation of a civil airliner, and could carry 154 passengers or 76 casualties up to 3650 miles (5875 km) on its four turbofans. New types now began to arrive thick and fast, and in 1966 no less than three new transports entered service in the forms of the Lockheed Hercules four-turboprop short/medium-range tactical airlifter with accommodation for 92 troops or 64 paratroops, the Shorts Belfast four-turboprop heavy logistic freighter and the Hawker Siddeley Andover twin-turboprop light utility and tactical transport. The early 1960s were also notable for the advent of two important helicopter types, the Westland (Bristol) Belvedere and the Westland Wessex, for support of troops on the battlefield. The Belvedere was an all-British design with twin rotors, and entered service in 1961 though serving for only a few years at a time of rapid increment of helicopter capabilities. The Wessex was a British twin-turbine development of the Sikorsky S-58, an American type with a single piston engine, and could be fitted with light armament for the suppport of the troops it ferried about the battlefield. The Wessex was then complemented and finally supplanted by the Puma HC.1, the British version of the helicopter developed by Aerospatiale in France and then produced jointly by Aerospatiale and Westland after the inter-governmental agreement of April 1967 for co-production of three helicopters, namely the Puma in the all-weather tactical transport role, the

The Wessex was replaced in frontline service by the Anglo-French Puma. The Puma is an all-weather tactical transport and provides medium lift capability to the army

Aerospatiale Gazelle in the scout and light attack roles, and the Westland Lynx (army version) in the armed tactical and anti-tank roles. In its battlefield role the Puma can carry 16 fully equipped infantrymen or six casualties, and its great advantages over the Wessex are all-weather avionics, a higher power-to-weight ratio for more sprightly performance, and a more modern design offering greater aerial agility as well as improved resistance to the effects of ground fire.

By the spring of 1975 Air Support Command comprised Nos 38 and 46 Groups, the former constituting the tactical air-support element for the army and the latter the transport element. No 38 Group comprised nine squadrons in the form of No 1 Squadron with Harrier GR.3 close support aircraft at RAF Wittering, Nos 6 and 54 Squadrons with Jaguar GR.1 attack aircraft at RAF Coltishall, Nos 33 and 230 Squadrons with Puma HC.1 tactical helicopters at RAF Odiham, No 42 Squadron with Phantom FGR.2 multi-role fighters at RAF Coningsby, No 72 Squadron with Wessex HC.2 helicopters at Odiham, and Nos 45 and 58 Squadrons with Hunter FGA.9 ground-attack fighters at RAF Wittering. No 46 Group comprised 12 squadrons in the form of No 10 Squadron with VC10 C.1s at RAF Brize Norton, Nos 24, 30, 36, 47, 48, and 70 Squadrons with the Hercules C.1 at RAF Lyneham. No 46 Squadron with Andover C.1s at RAF Thorney Island, No 53 Squadrons with Belfast C.1s at Brize Norton, Nos 99 and 511 Squadrons with Britannia C.1s and C.2s at Lyneham, and No 216 Squadron with Comet C.4s at Lyneham.

Above: Entering service during the mid-1960s the Hawker Siddeley Andover twin-turboprop provided the air force with a light utility and tactical transport aircraft

Left: The Shorts Belfast four-turboprop aircraft entered service in 1966 in the role of a heavy logistic freighter. Ten of these aircraft were procured by the RAF

UN

Left: A Westland Whirlwind operating in Cyprus as part of Britain's contribution to the United Nations' peacekeeping force

Throughout the period these transport aircraft were among the most heavily employed of RAF assets. Some of the transports' operations were occasioned by a British response to natural disasters, such as those in British Honduras and Morocco during 1960 and that in Kenya during 1961. More often, however, there was a natural military requirement. At times this was in support of organisations such as the United Nations, whose 'peacekeeping' force in the Congo was afforded Transport Command support from July 1960, but more often it was related to the military operations of the UK or its allies. Typical of the latter is the RAF's successful 1961 effort in bolstering Kuwait, whose new-found independence was threatened by Iraqi aggression. In response, British forces were moved into Kuwait fron the UK, Cyprus and Bahrain, while two Hunter squadrons flew in from Aden and Canberras arrived from West Germany and Cyprus. This complete force was supported logistically by transport aircraft from the UK, Kenya, Aden and the Far East. In fact it was the difficulty of the operation that persuaded the British government that the RAF's air transport capability was overtaxed to the extent that orders were placed for the VC10 and Belfast.

In May 1962 a squadron of Hunters was stationed in Thailand after incursions by Laotian troops, and supplies for this small force were ferried in by four-engined Handley Page Hastings and Beverley transports. Towards the end of the year the same squadron was shifted to the protectorate of Brunei in the northern part of Borneo, where a rebellion had broken out. Other air transport assets deployed to Brunei were Scottish Aviation Pioneers which had been based on the island of Labuan on anti-piracy patrols, and Beverleys and Belvederes from Singapore: troops were flown in on the larger transports and then moved into action by the Pioneers and Belvederes.The Brunei situation was soon brought under control, but a conflict of more serious implications then flared elsewhere in Borneo as Indonesia's opposition to the concept of a Malaysian Federation erupted into guerrilla attacks on Sabah and Sarawak.

Below: A Westland Wessex flies over the lush Malaysian countryside in support of British troops

As the violence in Borneo became worse, Beverleys began to fly British families out of Indonesia from September 1963. The confrontation with Indonesia lasted until 1966, during which time British and Commonwealth forces were supplied directly by Wessex helicopters and indirectly by Beverleys and Argosies which air-dropped vital supplies. In the course of the small but bitter land operations Singapore-based Canberras were used to deliver air attacks, and a detachment of V-bombers was based at Singapore.

Other troop deployments carried out by the RAF during the early 1960s included British Guiana in 1963, Kenya and Uganda in 1964, Mauritius in 1965, and most seriously Cyprus and Aden. The outbreak of civil war in Cyprus, which had become independent in 1960 and which provided the bases for the Near East Air Force at Akrotiri and Dhekelia, resulted initially in the dispatch of substantial reinforcements to the island. In March 1964 the UN assumed responsibility for security on the island and the resultant multinational peacekeeping force was thereafter supported by RAF transport aircraft and helicopters. The early 1960s also witnessed the beginning of a major effort in Aden to oust the British, who had already announced their intention of granting the region its independence, while also securing the superiority of the Communist party. A significant group campaign was launched by the British even as the campaign spread into a terrorist effort in Aden proper, and the RAF played a key part in these operations in the Radfan mountains behind Aden. Hunters were used for ground attack, Avro Shackletons for bombing and Belvederes for logistic support as well as tactical troop movement. The communist effort in the Adeni hinterland was largely contained, even when the Yemen intervened along the northern frontier, but by the mid-1960s the main communist effort was being made in Aden as the British completed plans for their withdrawal, which was finally accomplished in 1967 with Hercules transports flying out the last elements.

Between 1967 and 1975 the world situation of the UK was transformed out of all recognition as the nation withdrew from virtually all of its global commitments and turned increasingly towards a European commitment within the economico-political context of

the European Community and the strategic context of the NATO alliance. In these years British forces were finally withdrawn from Aden, as mentioned above, and also from Libya, Bahrain and with a few small-scale exceptions the Far East. The UK retained treaty obligations to support some of these nations in the event of aggression against them, but increasingly the British military emphasis shifted towards Europe, and the furthest deployments envisaged for all but very small forces were Cyprus and Gibraltar. Crisis situations later expanded this commitment to include Belize and the Falkland Islands, but these requirements were far from uppermost in the minds of the planners of the early 1970s.

As may well be imagined, these far-flung operations connected with the gradual withdrawal of the UK from its previous Imperial role occupied a large part of the nation's military strength. The services most directly affected were the Army and the Air Force, the latter in direct support of the British and allied forces in the field (or deploying to meet possible emergencies) as well as in the indirect support of the whole British effort with transport aircraft plying the lines of communications to trouble-spots. But though this effort demanded the attentions of substantial manpower and aircraft strengths, the RAF consistently refused to let its most advanced aircraft be redeployed to areas away from Europe, where in any event they would not have been suitable in operational terms.

Unhappily, however, the retention of the most advanced aircraft for European commitments meant relatively little as this was the RAF's period of lowest strength in qualitative as well as quantitative terms. This should not be construed as meaning that the service did not formulate advanced requirements or that British industry could not meet these requirements at the technical level, but rather that political procrastination and the heavy-handed bureaucracy so slowed the process that the aircraft were a long time coming, and often overtaken by shifting political beliefs and deteriorating economic conditions. The saddest case in point is the BAC TSR-2, an ambitious type that pushed the British state of the art to its limit, but which was cancelled in 1964 by a newly installed Labour administration for purely political reasons masquerading as economic factors.

A Shackleton of 205 Squadron operating from Gan during 1967. The Shackletons were deployed to the area to supply bomber support to the ground forces

XR219

Above: The cancellation of the TSR-2 project was a crushing blow for Britain's aircraft industry and left the RAF with a major lack of strike capabilities

Left: The elegant but ill-fated British Aircraft Company TSR-2 takes off on a test flight. The project pushed the limits of technology, and offered great potential, but design problems and soaring costs gave the then Labour government the excuse to cancel it

The origins of the TSR-2 may be found in the period when the RAF switched its V-bombers to the low-altitude penetration role. Even before this, the RAF had come to the opinion that while the V-bombers offered the maximum deterrent value, their combat lives would be short, as their bases would, in all probability, disappear in a Soviet first strike just after (it was hoped) the majority of the aircraft had become airborne for their attacks on Soviet targets. Bomber Command therefore planned for Low-level tactical strike by the rest of its aircraft using conventional and nuclear weapons. The NATO operating scenario of the period suggested that second-line bases in western France might survive the initial Soviet onslaught and thus provide the springboards from which Bomber Command could maintain its offensive task. What was needed, therefore, was a bomber that could operate effectively from such airfields: in short a STOL strike bomber capable of operating over long ranges at high speeds and low level. The aeroplane that emerged from this requirement was the TSR-2, an elegant and far-sighted design that involved much of the British aircraft industry and offered great potential, albeit at considerable cost. The airframe offered distinct aerodynamic and structural challenges, and so too did the engines and the advanced nav/attack system, while there was also the key challenge of integrating all the disparate components into an effective weapon system. As was inevitable in a programme of such size and complexity, there were development delays and cost overruns, but the first prototype was just beginning to reveal its capability when the whole programme was cancelled as the Labour government switched the emphasis of RAF operations entirely to the defensive. At the same time most other advanced aircraft programmes were cancelled.

It has never been revealed whether or not the RAF could really have afforded the TSR-2 and all its costly infrastructure without premature scrapping of the V-bomber force. In the short term the scrapping of the TSR-2 and all other advanced warplane projects resulted not just in the loss of a superb warplane but also in the decimation of a sophisticated industrial capacity. As an alternative to the TSR-2 the government ordered from the USA a variant of the General Dynamics F-111, but this swing-wing type was so delayed in development that its order too was finally cancelled by the British government.

MORE LIMITED HORIZONS: TOWARDS A TACTICAL RAF

By 1975 the RAF was well along the path towards a Eurocentric deployment and tasking. Such a move had been presaged in the 1968 amalgamation of RAF Bomber and Fighter Commands as RAF Strike Command, which was increased in November 1969 by the absorption of Coastal Command. Thus Strike Command became responsible for defensive and offensive air operations conducted as such, while Air Support Command was tasked with those air operations directly associated with ground operations by the Army. The RAF was being thoroughly overhauled in this period, and in June 1968 the flying training and technical training branches of the service were combined as RAF Training Command.

The technical situation facing the new commands, and especially Strike and Air Support Commands as the core of the RAF's offensive/defensive capability, was daunting: the USSR was in the throes of a major improvement of its forces in both numerical and technical terms, thereby offering a considerably more serious threat to the Western alliance, while the RAF was in common with the other British services being effectively starved of the financial support that would allow not only the needed expansion but also the purchase of new aircraft types with which to meet the Soviet threat.

The V-bombers and their in-flight refuelling tankers were the responsibility of Strike Command's No 1 Group. By the end of 1970 the pure strike elements comprised ten squadrons based in the UK: the offensive capability was vested in five squadrons of Vulcan B.2s and two squadrons of Buccaneer S.2s, and this capability was enhanced by three squadrons of Victor tankers. As noted above, the Buccaneer had originally been produced for the Fleet Air Arm, and was a carrierborne strike aeroplane powered in its original Buccaneer S.1 form by two de Havilland Gyron turbojets. The aeroplane was decidedly underpowered with this engine, but was nevertheless a superb low-level strike machine with transonic performance and, perhaps just as importantly, provided a smooth low-level ride that allowed its crew to fly long-range missions without that degradation of crew performance associated with bumpiness-induced fatigue. With the run-down of the Royal Navy's larger carriers the Fleet Air Arm lost its ability to operate conventional fixed-wing aircraft, and most of its 84 improved Buccaneer S.2s with Rolls-Rolls Spey turbofans were reallocated to the RAF as partial replacements for the cancelled TSR-2. In 1968 the much delayed British version of the General Dynamics F-111 was also cancelled, and to replace this lost capability the RAF ordered 43 new Buccaneers.

Both the TSR-2 and F-111 had offered superb operational qualities, and it was with considerable misgivings that the service received its first ex-naval Buccaneers. These misgivings soon faded as RAF aircrews came to grips with their 'new' machines: the payload/range, sturdiness and suberb ride all came to be appreciated, and with the delivery of the additional aircraft between 1970 and 1976 the service knew that it had an excellent strike platform. The type is still in service, and indeed the RAF now wishes that it had been able to receive more Buccaneers, and that in-service machines could be updated electronically to remain in more than useful service into the next century.

The growth of the Buccaneer force allowed two RAF Germany squadrons to turn in their elderly Canberras for more versatile Buccaneers, now equipped with the excellent Martel air-to-surface missile. Resulting from one of the first European interna-

Previous page: A Hawker Siddeley Buccaneer S.2 of No 12 Squadron skims the waves during a maritime patrol. Although it was first flown as early as 1958, the Buccaneer will continue in service well into the 1990s

tional collaborative projects, the Martel was produced by the UK and France in two variants. One is a radar-homing type to deal with hostile air-defence emitters, and the other had TV guidance. This latter features a TV camera in its nose, pictures being relayed to the Buccaneer's rear-seat operator, who can then guide the missile right onto its target with a very high degree of accuracy.

During the early 1970s the V-bomber force was also revised. The two Vulcan B.2 squadrons based in Cyprus were recalled to the UK in 1970, the Victor SR.2s strategic reconnaisance aircraft were converted to tankers, and some Vulcan B.2s were converted to assume the strategic reconnaissance role. It was planned that all the Victor tankers should have been retired by 1982, but their utility at a time when the need for in-flight refuelling is becoming all the more important has meant that they have been retained in fruitful service up to the present, with a retirement date in the 1990s now probable.

It was clear by the late 1960s that the RAF needed new fighters for Strike Command's No 11 Group. Though well liked by its pilots for its excellent flying qualities, the Lightning was no more than adequate as an interceptor, and the Hunter was obsolete even as a fighter-bomber. The ideal solution, given the lack of a

A Lightning of No 11 Squadron stands in readiness as part of No 1 Group, providing air defence for the UK during the early 1980s

A Phantom FGR.2 of No 29 Squadron at RAF Coningsby is armed with Sidewinder air-to-air missiles. Behind the Sidewinders is a single Sparrow radar-guided air-to-air missile in final preparation for loading

British successor as a result of government indifference and parsimony, was an American type in the form of the legendary McDonnell (later McDonnell Douglas) F-4 Phantom II. This multi-role type could combine the interceptor and fighter-bomber roles, and in 1968 52 Phantom FG.1s were ordered. This was a derivative of the US Navy's F-4J with extensive revision for British equipment and Spey turbofans in place of the original General Electric J79 turbojets. Of the Phantom FG.1s 24 went to the Royal Navy, creating two multi-role squadrons for services on HMS Ark Royal, while the other formed the equipment of two Strike Command air-defence squadrons. A further development of the F-4J was ordered as the Phantom FGR.2, and the 118 examples of this multi-role fighter, ground-attack and reconnaissance type have served exclusively with the RAF: by 1975 there were three Strike Command and four RAF Germany squadrons equipped with the variant, and by 1982 the RAF fleet had been augmented by ex-naval Phantoms, the new balance being two squadrons in West Germany and five in the UK. In 1982 the US supplied an additional squadron of F.4Js to allow the UK to maintain NATO need and meet the Falklands requirement. The type's tasking was by now mainly air defence with Sidewinder heat-seeking and Sparrow semi-active radar homing air-to-air missiles plus an underfuselage pod containing a 20-mm rotary-barrel cannon, but ground attack and reconnaissance remained important secondary tasks, the former with up to 16,000 lb (7257 kg) of disposable stores and the latter with an underfuselage multi-sensor reconnaissance pod.

No 11 Group's air-defence role with just a comparatively small force of Lightnings and Phantoms was exceptionally difficult, even with ground-based radars to provide the data on which ground controllers could compute interception courses. An expansion of this capability was offered by the RAF's airborne early warning aircraft. Introduced in 1971, these comprised a group of 12 Avro Shackleton maritime patrol aircraft, already 20 years old after protracted service with No 18 Group, converted to Shackleton AEW.3 standard by the addition of ATS-20 surveillance radar. This radar was of greater vintage even than the Shackleton, for it had been designed in the Second World War, had been updated for continued viability after that war, and was now stripped out of the Fleet Air Arm's Fairley Gannet aircraft when these were retired during the gradual elimination of the Royal Navy's large aircraft-carriers. Patrolling beyond the

Phantoms of No 111 Squadron on the flight line at RAF Leuchars in Scotland in 1980. The front aircraft is fitted with long-range tanks, and Sidewinder missiles are positioned in front of several aircraft waiting to be loaded

range of ground-based radars, the radar-carrying Shackletons provided invaluable if limited warning of impending attacks and, as a result of the skill of their crews, a useful control capability for the responding fighters. Thus the Shackletons were genuine 'force multipliers'. The aircraft were intended only as interim AEW platforms pending the development of an advanced airborne warning and control system aeroplane, the AEW.3 development of the British Aerospace Nimrod maritime patrol and anti-submarine type.

A complement to the Buccaneer and Phantom was provided by a uniquely British aeroplane, the Hawker Siddeley (now British Aerospace) Harrier. This entered service in 1969 as the world's first operational warplane with vertical take-off and landing (VTOL) capability. The Harrier was derived from the P.1127 research and Kestrel pre-production types, and uses four swivelling nozzles to vector the thrust of its Bristol (now Rolls-Royce) Pegasus turbofan. These nozzles are located two on each side of the fuselage: the forward pair channels the cold air from the fan stage of

A Lossiemouth-based Shackleton AEW.2 on deployment to RAF Gibraltar. Equipped with the ATS-20 surveillance radar which was developed during the Second World War, these aircraft were replaced by the Boeing E-3 Sentry in July 1990

12
27

Previous page main picture: Harrier GR.3s of No 1 Squadron on deployment to Norway. The introduction of the Harrier freed the RAF from conventional runways and the Harrier GR.3 has for many years successfully operated in the frozen wastes of northern Norway, as well as in the battle for the Falklands and in the jungles of Belize

Previous page left inset: A flight of three Harrier GR.3s of No 3 Squadron during a training mission

Previous page right inset: Harrier GR.1s operating from a wooded hide. The Harrier's unique ability to take off and land on short stretches of ground has played a major role in the development of close support for ground forces

the engine, while the rear pair channels the hot gases from the engine's turbine core. The pilot has a simple control lever to rotate the nozzles in unison so that with the nozzles in the position to duct the engine thrust straight down the Harrier is driven up into the air, where the nozzles can be angled back to shift the thrust steadily rearward and so provide an increasing measure of forward thrust so that the aeroplane translates into wingborne flight. For a vertical landing the procedure is reversed, and it is also possible to angle the nozzles slightly forward to provide braking thrust. In practice the vertical take-off is seldom used because this limits the Harrier's maximum take-off weight to slightly less than the thrust of the engine: the standard practice is therefore short take-off and vertical landing (STOVL) in which the heavily laden Harrier accelerates for perhaps 250 yards (230 m) with the nozzles to the rear, allowing the wings to generate a useful quantity of lift before the nozzles are shifted directly downward to hurl the aeroplane into the air, where the nozzles are again turned to the rear.

The great operational significance of the Harrier was and is that it removes this important close air-support aeroplane from NATO's increasingly vulnerable airfields, the standard operating procedure being off-base deployment to a forest clearing, sheltered fields, etc, with each aeroplane supported by a few technicians and vehicles with fuel, armament and other essential supplies. Such sites can be changed frequently, even between missions, and are so difficult to detect that they are relatively invulnerable. This means that a dispersed Harrier force can continue to operate in the field for several days even if NATO's airfields are totally destroyed.

Only limited production has been undertaken to provide a force of two operational squadrons based in West Germany and one squadron in the UK. The original Harrier GR.1 was soon converted to GR.3 standard with more power, a laser ranger and marked target seeker in a revised nose, and a radar-warning receiver in the tail. The Harrier is cleared to lift some 5000 lb (2268 kg) of stores but in trials has operated successfully with upwards of 8000 lb (3629 kg). Generally two 30-mm cannon are carried in under-fuselage strakes that serve as lift-improvement devices by trapping gas reflected from the ground during VTOL. The rest of the armament load can include a pair of AIM-9 Sidewinder air-to-air missiles for self-defence, plus a wide assortment of modern air-to-surface weapons including pods for unguided rockets, free-fall and retarded bombs, cluster bombs able to release a cloud of submunitions, and laser-guided bombs that home onto a target 'illuminated' by a laser designator of the right frequency in another aeroplane or helicopter, or even in the hands of a soldier on the ground. The Harrier can also operate in the reconnaissance role, for it possesses an oblique camera in the nose as standard equipment, and can also be fitted with a multi-sensor reconnaissance pod carried on one of the four underwing hardpoints.

Right: Three GR.3s from No 3 Squadron are seen here armed with air-to-ground unguided rockets

With its twin Rolls-Royce Adour turbofans fully prepared, this Anglo-French SEPECAT Jaguar prepares to take off

Operating in parallel with the Harrier but in the attack role against targets deeper behind the front line is the SEPECAT Jaguar. This is another collaborative project, again between British and French partners but in this instance Breguet and the British Aircraft Corporation, now parts of Dassault and British Aerospace respectively. The type originated from separate British and French requirements for a supersonic flight and weapons trainer. The two governments then saw the economic and technical advantages of combined development, which was thus entrusted to the SEPECAT consortium created to design, develop and produce an aeroplane based ultimately on the Br.121 concept. Rolls-Royce and Turbomeca also collaborated to produce the aeroplane's superb Adour turbofan. What emerged from the programme was a type certainly capable of use in the original design concept role, but also possessing such potential in the operational role that this latter has predominated in production contracts. The Jaguar GR.1 began to enter British (mainly RAF Germany) service during 1973, and has become a classic attack aeroplane of its period. One of the primary tactical advantages possessed by the Jaguar is, surprisingly enough, its lack of radar: this means that the aeroplane is electronically 'silent' apart from its radar altimeter, and therefore hard for modern air-defence systems to detect. Despite this lack of radar the Jaguar is still an all-weather type through its highly advanced nav/attack system, whose computer and inertial navigation system allow the aeroplane to fly a pre-planned course of such accuracy that the pilot can make a first-pass attack using his head-up display and

laser ranger and marked target seeker. The Jaguar can deliver tactical nuclear weapons in addition to the same basic types of ordnance as the Harrier, and its weapon-carriage capability is much enhanced by the aeroplane's configuration with a high wing and stalky landing gear, which permit the loading of a bulky store under the fuselage as well as on the four underwing hardpoints. Like the Harrier, the Jaguar has been steadily upgraded in capability with more power and improved electronics, the latter including a radar-warning receiver, and flare and chaff launchers. The Harriers of RAF Germany are still tasked with attack and nuclear strike, with secondary reconnaissance responsibility via a pod, while British-based Jaguars are used mainly for tactical reconnaissance.

Main picture: A head-on shot of a Jaguar GR.1 that is carrying an asymmetric load

Left inset: Carrying 2 × 1000 lb (450 kg) bombs and 2 external fuel tanks, this Jaguar GR.1 of No 226 Squadron cuts its way through the early morning air

Right inset: Based at RAF Coltishall, this Jaguar GR.1 of 54 Squadron is carrying four 1000 lb (450 kg) bombs and two 260 gallon (1200 litre) fuel tanks

As noted previously, the Shackleton was to be replaced as an AEW type by a version of the Nimrod, itself the successor to the Shackleton in the maritime patrol role on No 18 Group of Strike Command. The Nimrod was not entirely a new design even when it entered service, for its basic layout and structure were derived from those of the Comet C.4, though heavily modified for a powerplant of four Spey turbofans and a 'double-bubble' fuselage with a pressurised upper lobe for the 12-man crew and an unpressurised lower lobe (or rather pannier) accommodating the long and capacious weapon bay. At a time when other major air forces were operating or developing turboprop-powered maritime patrollers, the RAF's decision to opt for turbofan power was both courageous and far-sighted: the availability of four engines provides the power for heavy take-offs and high-speed transit to the operational area, where two engines can be shut down as an economy measure during the long hours of low-speed patrol in the designated area. The airframe was also capacious enough for the mass of specialised equipment needed for the Nimrod's primary mission, this equipment including search radar, a magnetic anomaly detector, a sniffer for diesel exhaust fumes, electronic support measures equipment, and a large number of active/passive sonobuoys for release into the sea. These sonobuoys listen for sounds of submarine activity and transmit their information to an advanced data-processing system tied into the computerised tactical system that co-ordinate acoustic and other

sensors to produce a scenario on which the crew can base useful tactical decisions.

Orders for the Nimrod MR.1 totalled 46, and the first of 43 actually delivered began to enter service in October 1969 for service with one Malta-based and four UK-based squadrons. The three others were completed as Nimrod R.1 electronic intelligence aircraft, highly classified machines that roam the aerial periphery of potential enemies' land areas 'listening' for electronic emissions that can reveal vital information about all types of electro-magnetic emitters. Some 32 Nimrod MR.1s were later revised to a Nimrod MR.2 standard that totally transformed the already high operational capability of the type by adding an inertial navigation system and a totally new suite of sensors and tactical equipment better able to deal with the problems associated with detecting, tracking, identifying and, if required, attacking the increasingly sophisticated submarines capable of high underwater speed, diving depth and endurance.

No 18 Group also controls the RAF's search-and-rescue (SAR) helicopter force. Through most of the 1970s this force comprised Wessex twin-turbine helicopters, but from August 1978 the emphasis shifted towards the Westland Sea King HAR.3, a specialised variant of the Royal Navy's Sea King anti-submarine helicopter. Like the Wessex, this has twin turboshafts and is derived from an American original, the Sikorsky S-61 that serves the US Navy as the Sh-3 anti-submarine and general-purpose helicopter.

Above: A Westland Whirlwind helicopter powered by a single Rolls-Royce Gnome engine is used to lift a 'downed pilot' during a training exercise

Left: The successor to the Whirlwind was the more powerful Westland Wessex. It was powered by twin Rolls-Royce Gnome engines

Opposite top: Armed with Sidewinder missiles for air defence, this Nimrod MR.2 is on watch for Soviet surface and sub-surface vessels. It is equipped with the Thorn EMI Searchwater advanced computer-assisted radar, acoustic processing and a tactical battle computer

Opposite bottom: The Nimrod is a development of the Comet C.4 powered by four Spey turbofans. It has a crew of 12

THE ROYAL AIR FORCE TODAY

As the RAF celebrates its 75th Anniversary the service is well into the process of 'drawdown' (a euphemism for size reduction) in the wake of the ending of the so-called Cold War and the dissolution of the Warsaw Pact. Between 1991 and 1995 the strength of the RAF is set to fall from around 88,000 to below 74,000. The associated cutbacks of squadrons and bases continues to cause the demise of such famous units as Nos 19, 20, 42, 55, 60, 74, and 92 Squadrons. RAF Gutersloh and RAF Wildenrath in Germany, along with RAF Abingdon and RAF Hullavington are among the airfields marked down for closure. At no time since 1939 has the overall manning level of the RAF been smaller than it is now.

While the service has palpably shrunk in quantitative terms, the same is not necessarily so qualitatively, as can be gauged by the RAF's impressive performance during the Gulf War of 1991. As well as being the RAF's 75th Anniversary, 1993 also marks the effective conclusion of an extensive modernisation programme that commenced during the 1980s. The programme has introduced some momentous advances in terms of both service hardware and capability. New combat aircraft types now deployed include the Panavia Tornado F.3 and BAe Harrier GR.5/7, along with a significant strengthening of the RAF's vital range-extending tanker assets in the shape of VC10K and Tristar. Equally massive progress has been brought about in the area of Command, Control and Communication (C^3) thanks to the replacement of the pre-jet age Shackleton AEW.2 by the Boeing Sentry AEW.1 in the air, while ground-based C^3 systems have also undergone a major upgrade with the introduction of the new UK Air Defence Ground Environment network. New weapons introduced include the runway-denying JP322, BAe Dynamic's extremely effective ALARM missile, used to suppress enemy anti-aircraft defences and the UK Paveway II laser-guided 1,000 lb high explosive bomb; all of which were used to such great effect in the recent Gulf War.

Mention of the Gulf War leads, naturally enough, to a brief review of the RAF's role in the conflict; an action in which the service played a pivotal part, both at the outset in defence of Saudi Arabia, and later, in helping to win the necessary Coalition air supremacy required before their ground forces could dare move against the Iraqis.

Small as the RAF's contribution may have been in numbers of aircraft and personnel, the operational effort mounted by the service played a disproportionately large part in neutralising the far from insignificant Iraqi Air Force. Indeed, it is a striking fact that out of a total of around 2,400 Coalition aircraft employed either in combat or support, the RAF's contribution amounted to just 160 in-theatre aircraft, or approximately 7 per cent of the total.

The Gulf Crisis commenced at 2 a.m. local time on 2 August 1990 with the simultaneous thrust of three Iraqi Republican Guard armoured divisions across the Kuwaiti borders, coupled with the taking

Previous page: An early Panavia Tornado IDS of the Tri-national Tornado Training Establishment based at RAF Cottesmore. It is shown in a typical long-range, low-level strike configuration with eight bombs, two 330 gallon (1500 litre) fuel tanks and ECM pods

Right: A Tornado GR.1 of No 15 Squadron makes a low-level flight over wooded countryside

Opposite: The Tornado can climb almost vertically even when heavily loaded. This Tornado GR.1 of No 15 Squadron has 330 gallon (1500 litre) fuel tanks, a Boz chaff dispenser and a Sky Shadow ECM pod

EM
XV

of Kuwait City by air and seaborne elements of Iraq's Republican Guard's Special Forces. International condemnation was instant and unambiguous with the United Nations' Security Council demanding an Iraqi withdrawal from Kuwait less than a day after the initial Iraqi incursion.

Diplomatic activity notwithstanding, the threat now facing the other Gulf States, particularly Saudi Arabia, was very real. Saddam Hussein's initial Kuwaiti invasion force of around 100,000 troops, backed by 1,250 tanks, were already being reinforced with divisions of the regular Iraqi Army. Alarmed, the Saudi Arabian Government appealed for help in defending their borders. On 8 August President Bush announced the deployment of US forces to the area followed the same day by a similar commitment from the British Government.

The key to countering this potentially dangerous situation was to deploy Coalition defensive forces with the greatest rapidity and, here, Air Power alone had the mobility to respond in a timely fashion. On 9 August, the British Government disclosed that it was dispatching squadrons of Tornado F.3s and Jaguar GR.1s, each consisting of 12 aircraft, plus 3 Nimrod MR.2s. Two days later the Tornado F.3s, taken from Nos 8 and 29 Squadrons departed RAF Akrotiri in Cyprus for Dhahran, Saudi Arabia, where, within two hours of arrival, they were back in the air flying the first of many air defence patrols. Later on 11 August and continuing the next day came the initial Jaguar contingent, drawn from No 54 Squadron, RAF Coltishall, who with the help of No 101 Squadron tankers, staged through RAF Akrotiri on route for Thumrait in southern Oman.

Over the remaining months of 1990, the RAF strength in the Gulf area rose from the initial 24 combat aircraft, plus the three Nimrod maritime patrollers, to a total of 81 combat aircraft, comprising an additional 45 Tornado GR.1As, plus 6 Tornado F.3s. Further aircraft sent to the area during this period included 1 Nimrod, a mixed tanker force of VC10Ks, Victors and a single Tristar numbering 17 in all, along with an in-theatre logistical transport element of 7 Hercules and tactical helicopter transport in the shape of 17 Chinooks and 19 Pumas. Last, but not least, urgent communications flight and VIP transport was provided by a solitary HS125 based for the duration at Riyadh, Saudi Arabia. Mention must also be made of the mammoth, if largely unsung support provided by the UK-based transport squadrons, who flew some 13 million air miles and moved over 50,000 tonnes of freight into the Gulf area – figures that represent a work rate some six times the normal. The code name for the overall build-up of British military and naval forces in the Gulf was Operation Granby.

During this period, while the RAF's Tornado F.3s continued their defensive patrols over the Gulf and northern Saudi Arabia, efforts on the diplomatic front appeared to be making little if any progress. Saddam Hussein appeared to be growing ever more intransigent, calling on his people to prepare for the "Mother of all Wars". On 29 November 1990, United Nations Resolution 678 set 15 January as the date by which Iraq was to fully comply with earlier United Nations' calls thus giving Saddam Hussein nearly seven more weeks good will pause. During the early hours of 17 January 1991, the campaign to liberate Kuwait, code-named Operation Desert Storm, commenced.

The first and by far the most important phase of Operation Desert Storm was the campaign to establish air supremacy over the terrain to be regained from the Iraqis. To do this meant destroying the Iraqi Air Force's ability to fight, which, in turn, implied the need to either destroy any aircraft that might be concealed in hardened shelters, or to destroy the runways from which they needed to

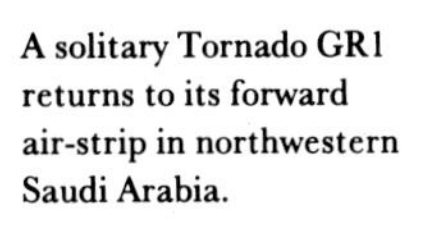
A solitary Tornado GR1 returns to its forward air-strip in northwestern Saudi Arabia.

The STRENGTH OF THE ROYAL AIRFORCE
(FRONT LINE UNITS ONLY)

Unit	Base	Aircraft
STRIKE/ATTACK		
9 Sqn	RAF Bruggen	13 Tornado GR1
12 Sqn (Disbanding 1993)	RAF Lossiemouth	12 Buccaneer, 2 Hunter
14 Sqn	RAF Bruggen	13 Tornado GR1
17 Sqn	RAF Bruggen	13 Tornado GR1
27 Sqn (To Lossiemouth 1993)	RAF Marham	13 Tornado GR1 (Renumbering to No 12 Sqn)
31 Sqn	RAF Bruggen	13 Tornado GR1
208 Sqn (Disbanding 1994)	RAF Lossiemouth	12 Buccaneer, 5 Hunter
617 Sqn (To Lossiemouth 1993)	RAF Marham	13 Tornado GR1
OFFENSIVE SUPPORT		
1 Sqn	RAF Wittering	14 Harrier
3 Sqn	RAF Laarbruch	15(13) Harrier
4 Sqn	RAF Laarbruch	14(13) Harrier
6 Sqn	RAF Coltishall	14 Jaguar
54 Sqn	RAF Coltishall	15 Jaguar
RECONNAISSANCE		
2 Sqn	RAF Marham	13 Tornado GR1A
13 Sqn	RAF Honington	13 Tornado GR1A
39 (1 PRU) Sqn	RAF Wyton	7(7) Canberra
41 Sqn	RAF Coltishall	14 Jaguar
51 Sqn	RAF Wyton	3 Nimrod R1
MARITIME PATROL		
120 Sqn		
201 Sqn	RAF Kinloss	30 Nimrod MR2
206 Sqn		
AIR DEFENCE		
5 Sqn	RAF Coningsby	13 Tornado F3
6 Wing RAF Regt	RAF West Raynham	Rapier (USAF) (To Honington 1994)
11 Sqn	RAF Leeming	13 Tornado F3
15 Sqn RAF Regt	RAF Leeming	Rapier
16 Sqn RAF Regt	RAF West Raynham	RAF Rapier Training Unit (To Honington 1994)
19 Sqn RAF Regt	RAF Brize Norton	Rapier (USAF) (To Honington 1994)
20 Sqn RAF Regt	RAF Honington	Rapier (USAF) (To Honington 1994)
23 Sqn	RAF Leeming	13 Tornado F3
25 Sqn	RAF Leeming	13 Tornado F3
26 Sqn RAF Regt	RAF Laarbruch	Rapier
27 Sqn RAF Regt	RAF Leuchars	Rapier
29 Sqn	RAF Coningsby	13 Tornado F3
37 Sqn RAF Regt	RAF Bruggen	Rapier
43 Sqn	RAF Leuchars	16 Tornado F3
48 Sqn RAF Regt	RAF Lossiemouth	Rapier
66 Sqn RAF Regt	RAF West Raynham	Rapier (USAF) (To Honington 1994)
111 Sqn	RAF Leuchars	16 Tornado F3
1339 Wing R Aux AF Regt	RAF Waddington	Skyguard/Oerlikon
2729 Sqn R Aux AF Regt	RAF Waddington	Skyguard/Oerlikon
2890 Sqn R Aux AF Regt	RAF Waddington	Skyguard/Oerlikon
AIRBORNE EARLY WARNING		
8 Sqn	RAF Waddington	7 Sentry AEW
TANKERS		
55 Sqn (Disbanding Oct 1993)	RAF Marham	8 Victor K2
101 Sqn	RAF Brize Norton	9 VC10 K2/K3
AIRBORNE RADIO RELAY		
115 Sqn	RAF Benson	7(4) Andover
EW TRAINING/RADAR CALIBRATION		
360 Sqn	RAF Wyton	11(10) Canberra
TARGET TOWING		
100 Sqn	RAF Wyton	12 Hawks
AIR TRANSPORT		
7 Sqn	RAF Odiham	18 Chinook, 1 Gazelle
10 Sqn	RAF Brize Norton	10 VC10 C1/C1K(AAR capability 1992/93)
18 Sqn	RAF Laarbruch	5 Chinook (and 5 Puma)
24 Sqn	RAF Lyneham	13 Hercules
30 Sqn	RAF Lyneham	13 Hercules
32 Sqn	RAF Northolt	12 HS125,4(8) Andover, 4 Gazelle
33 Sqn	RAF Odiham	12 Puma
47 Sqn	RAF Lyneham	11 Hercules
60 Sqn	RAF Benson	9 Wessex
70 Sqn	RAF Lyneham	12 Hercules
72 Sqn	RAF Aldergrove	15 Wessex
216 Sqn	RAF Brize Norton	8 Tristar K1/KC1/C2(Dual Role Tanker/Transport)
230 Sqn	RAF Aldergrove	15 Puma
The Queen's Flight	RAF Benson	3BAe 146, 2 Wessex

operate. This was easier said than done and required a considerable investment in aircraft, weapons and, above all, realistic aircrew training. Fortunately, the RAF had this prerequisite in the shape of the Tornado GR.1 and the men who flew it.

From the commencement of actual hostilities RAF Tornado GR.1s were in the forefront of Coalition efforts to gain air superiority. The Tornado GR.1 squadrons' task was twofold: (i) to destroy the enemy's air capability, and (ii) to destroy the enemy's ability to counter-attack. The latter task would involve suppressing enemy radar directed against ground-based anti-aircraft defences. As these were frequently to be found defending the most high value military installations, including airfields, both tasks needed to be carried out simultaneously. With their ability to carry a broad range of sensors and weapons at high speeds and low level, both day and night, the Tornado GR.1s went forth to crater runways and taxiways with their JP322s, or to intimidate the Iraqi radar operators into leaving their equipment shut down rather than chance having an ALARM missile fall upon them.

The importance of ALARM, still in its develop-

ment phase when the RAF took it to war, cannot be overstated. Unlike earlier US-developed anti-ground radar missiles such as Shrike and HARM, ALARM does not necessarily home directly for its target radar once located. In contrast to the American method of 'going for the jugular' (a technique that implies a missile launch from higher than tree-top level), ALARM is launched from 'on the deck'. From here, the missile boosts itself into the high stratosphere, whence it commences its parachute-retarded descent back to earth, listening out for the tell-tale signature of one or more pre-ordained types of enemy radar. On aquisition of its prey, the missile dispenses with its parachute and, employing the potential energy bestowed by altitude, heads off directly for the target radar. Onboard processor-aided inertial navigation ensures that the missile continues to home into its target even if the radar closes down. Clearly the above sequence of events can involve a significant number of minutes in time elapsed should the missile be pre-programmed to soar to its maximum altitude and loiter-descend. Thus, as long as the enemy is aware of the missile's potential capabilities, the simple suspicion that

The RAF's main air-defence aircraft is the Tornado ADV (Air Defence Variant). It is armed with four British Aerospace Sky Flash semi-active radar homing air-to-air missiles. The basic Tornado was lengthened by 4 ft (1.2 m) to accomodate the missiles and the Foxhunter radar

The sleek lines of the Tornado ADV are shown to perfection in this photograph. This aircraft was on a test flight from British Aerospace Warton at the time. When the Boeing E-3 enters service, the two aircraft will prove an extremely potent combination

ALARM is being used in the area is likely to provide a significant deterrent value. Because of the specialised crew training and aircraft modification requirements that went hand-in-hand with the deployment of this largely untested missile, only one unit, No 20 Squadron (subsequently disbanded, but then based at Tabuk in north-western Saudi Arabia) was to be equipped with ALARM. Some indication of the haste surrounding the use of ALARM in Desert Storm can be gathered from the fact that the RAF could only procure one hundred of these missiles before pre-production stocks were exhausted.

Regrettably, the spearheading of the Coalition air offensive by the Tornado GR.1s was not without cost since six of them were lost in combat, along with the lives of five brave aircrew. Significantly, all of these losses occurred during the first eight days of the air war, when the low-level attacks against enemy airfields were at their peak.

After some isolated attempts by Iraqi aircraft to engage incoming Coalition air strikes during the first week of the air campaign, the Iraqi Air Force effectively withdrew from further action. At around this time Coalition air strikes switched away from runway inhibiting missions to the destruction of hardened aircraft shelters, undertaken from medium level altitudes. The Iraqi response to this shift in Coalition tactics was very soon apparent when they flew around 120 of their most modern aircraft to refuges in neighbouring Iran. In all, only 35 Iraqi machines were to be shot down during the entire 43 days of Operation Desert Storm.

With the switch from runway 'killing' to medium altitude strikes against pin-point targets such as aircraft shelters, bridges and command centres, the Tornado GR.1 force found itself lacking the bombing precision that its US colleagues were enjoying thanks to their wider adoption of laser-guided weapons and laser designators. On 24 January it was announced that six Buccaneers would be deployed to the Gulf to serve in the laser designator role. These aircraft, along with a further six, were all drawn from the sole remaining Buccaneer Wing at RAF Lossiemouth and enabled the Tornado strike force

This illustration of the Boeing E-3 Airborne Warning and Control System (AWACS) has been retouched by an artist in the markings of the RAF

to switch from the use of relatively inaccurate free-fall bombs to the employment of laser-guided weapons. In practice, one Buccaneer would accompany two Tornado GR.1s, the responsibility for identifying and tracking the target with the laser designator lying with the Buccaneer's crew; the UK Paveway II bombs released by the Tornado pair were then guided onto the target by sensing the reflected laser energy. During the conflict Buccaneers flew more than 200 sorties, mostly in support of Tornado strikes. However, towards the close of hostilities, the Buccaneer crews devised tactics by which they could act as self-designators for their own Paveway against less hardened targets such as bridges. A handful of Tornado GR.1s were latterly equipped with the Thermal Imaging Airborne Laser Designator (TIALD) system that was still in the development stage.

One other aspect of the air war in which the Tornado strike force played a major part was that of providing tactical reconnaissance, including the seeking out of Iraq's highly mobile Scud missile launchers. This task fell to the Tornado GR.1a, six of which were based at Dhahran. Their infra-red sensing system feeding into a video recorder and data link provided both real-time and stored images of the ground below and to the side of the flight track at any time of the day or night. The GR.1a Gulf detachment flew 140 operational sorties during the conflict, working usually in pairs at low-level and at night.

Based at Muharraq at the northern tip of Bahrain during Desert Storm, the force of 12 Jaguars was put to a variety of tasks, ranging from close air support to strikes against Iraqi naval targets. Although constricted to daylight operations and to the southern sector of the war zone, the Jaguars, armed with 1,000 lb free-fall bombs, cluster weapons and rockets, acquitted themselves well, flying more then 600 combat missions in all.

Sometimes referred to as 'The Enablers', the RAF's locally-based tanker force flew more than 730 sorties during the war, off-loading 13,000 tonnes of jet fuel, about 75 per cent going to RAF recipients,

B

The joint British Aerospace/ McDonnell Douglas Harrier II has been designated the GR.5 by the RAF. It is seen here operated by No 233 Operational Conversion Unit, which is based at RAF Wittering

The Harrier GR.5 entered RAF service in 1988 and has since been given full night attack capability as the GR.7

with Coalition aircraft taking the rest. Typical of the tanker effort was that of the No 55 Squadron detachment of Victor K.2s, based at Muharraq. During the 43 day conflict, this unit of seven aircraft flew 299 sorties, with a peak of 14 sorties per day.

One other element of the RAF effort in the Gulf was that of the largely unsung but essential Support Helicopter Force that operated as an integral part of the British Army's 1st Division. Beside the peak strength of 17 Chinooks and 19 Pumas, the Support Helicopter Force was augmented by 12 Sea Kings of the Royal Navy; the whole force being deployed to the rapid transport of vital items to the front and casualty evacuation, if required, on the return trip. Early on during the final land war phase of the conflict, the capabilities of the force were to be tested in full when it was realised that prisoners of war were in fear of dying of exposure. Responding rapidly, a part of the force was tasked to alleviate the situation. Within the span of a few hours, the helicopters had airlifted around 100 tonnes of life-supporting supplies and brought back over 3,300 prisoners to an adequately stocked prison compound. Overall, the Support Helicopter Force notched up a total of more than 5,000 flying hours, carried 17,500 troops and 2,750,000 lb of freight and evacuated more than 300 casualties. All this was achieved while deploying over 1,000 miles of inhospitable desert.

During the hostilities the RAF flew more than 4,000 combat missions as well as 2,500 support missions. The weight of weapons expended is officially quoted as exceeding 3,000 tonnes, including some 6,000 bombs, of which 1,000 were laser-guided. Other offensive stores exhausted are listed as more than 100 JP322s, around 100 ALARM missiles and nearly 700 air-to-ground rockets.

In the immediate aftermath of the conflict elements of the RAF's Hercules transport and support helicopter force transferred from the Gulf area to Turkey, from where they flew mercy missions in aid of the Kurdish population of northern Iraq.

The one RAF contingent never granted the opportunity to display its prowess was that of the Dhahran-based Tornado F.3 fighter force. In total, these aircraft flew over 2,600 sorties during their detachment to the Gulf, of which just over 700 were flown during the Desert Storm period. So few contacts were made with Iraqi aircraft that no Tornado F.3 crew was to fire its 27 mm cannon, or release an air-to-air missile in anger.

Since the cease fire of 28 February 1991 that brought hostilities in the northern Gulf to a conclusion, Saddam Hussein has wasted no opportunities to test United Nation's resolve. Mounting persecu-

Above: BAe's big winged Harrier GR7 can deliver over four tonnes of weaponry day or night in all but the most adverse weather.

Left: Half of the RAF's original fleet of Lockheed Hercules have been lengthened at Marshall's of Cambridge by the addition of plugs in front of and behind the main wing section

Opposite: Caught near the top of a loop this Tornado GR1 is seen carrying two BAe Dynamics' ALARM missiles under its fuselage, flanked by fuel tanks and electronic warfare pods outboard.

RAF ground crew prepare a Jaguar GR1 for its next sortie. Too frequently overlooked, much of the glamorous end result achieved depends directly on the immense, if unspectacular efforts of these unsung technicians.

tion of the Kurds in northern Iraq and similar acts against the Marsh Arabs in the south of the country led, in July 1992, to the imposition of 'no fly' zones from which Iraqi military aircraft were prohibited; the zones extending north from the 38th Parallel and south from the 32nd Parallel. During the autumn of 1992, a six-aircraft detachment of Tornado GR.1s returned to Saudi Arabia and it was this element forming part of an 80 strike and 30 support aircraft force that attacked an array of anti-aircraft installations on 14 January 1993

The Panavia Tornado, developed and produced jointly under British, West German and Italian interests, forms the backbone of today's RAF strike capability. The rationale was the need to counter any Soviet aggression against Western Europe with hard-hitting attacks on the chokepoints through which the Soviets would have to channel reinforcements, logistic supplies, ammunition etc., and on the Soviet's command nerve centres. The type had to be able to operate from damaged airfields or from lengths of motorway, to carry a substantial warload of diverse but modern weapons, to operate over long ranges at very high speed at very low level, and to

undertake first-pass attacks with pinpoint accuracy. The requirement was extremely demanding, yet resulted in the design of a singularly compact aeroplane. This has variable-geometry wings which provide maximum area and lift in the upswept position for take-off, medium area and low drag for fuel-economical cruising flight, and minimum area and drag for low-level supersonic flight over the target area. The wings are well provided with high-lift devices to enhance lift at low speeds for take-off and landing, and the extremely compact turbofans have thrust-reversers to enhance the Tornado's STOL capability. With the exception of two 27-mm cannon, the Tornado's armament is all carried externally, and some 18,000 lb (8165 kg) of stores can be carried on the aeroplane's nine hardpoints: under the fuselage one centreline and two tandem pairs, and under each wing two units designed to swivel and thus remain aligned with the ambient airflow for minimum drag no matter what angle of sweep is selected. These hardpoints can carry virtually every Western air-dropped weapon ranging from simple free-fall and retarded bombs, via rocket-launcher pods and free-fall cluster bombs, to the whole range

The Falklands campaign highlighted the need for long-range refuelling. Here a Victor K2 tanker of No 57 Squadron (based at RAF Marham) refuels a Nimrod Mk 2. The Nimrod fleet was given an inflight refuelling capability during the Falklands campaign

Chinook helicopters can carry a payload of 21,000 lb (9525 kg) at a range of 250 miles (400 km), which is almost four times the capability of the Puma helicopter. This Chinook is flown by No 18 Squadron

Right: RAF Chinooks stationed in the UK regularly deploy to Europe in support of NATO forces

of powered and unpowered guided weapons, as well as tactical nuclear weapons. All such weapons would in themselves be comparatively ineffective if their launch platform could not reach the target area accurately and safely, and in this department too the Tornado truly excels. The flight-control system is centred on a fly-by-wire system in which a computer interprets the pilot's control column movements and sends electronic commands to the actuators powering the control surfaces to produce an optimum response relevant to the Tornado's flight situation and loading. For navigation the Tornado has an inertial navigation system, Doppler navigation system, a main terrain-following radar: these allow fully automatic flight via selected waypoints at very low level, the pilot selecting the level of ride comfort (response to turbulence) that best suits him and his rear-seat systems operator in relation to the speed and height flown. For the attack proper the pilot uses data from a number of sensors (including the main radar, laser ranger and marked target seeker and any podded optronic systems) displayed on his head-up display, while the rear-seater monitors the performance of the whole system and supervises the defensive electronics, which include an inbuilt radar-warning receiver and a variety of podded systems including electronic countermeasures and chaff/flare dispensers.

The Tornado first flew in 1974, but the final development of the type to a level where service deliveries were possible took several years, and it was 1980 before the Tri-National Training

Below: The Handley Page Victor entered service with the Royal Air Force more than 30 years ago. The Victor tanker force is operated by No 55 Squadron at RAF Marham due to close in 1993

Above: A reconnaissance Jaguar from No 41 Squadron is prepared for flight by a ground crew at RAF Lossiemouth. They are wearing NBC (Nuclear Biological Chemical Warfare) protective clothing

Left: This Lockheed Hercules C1P, along with its RAF Lyneham based brothers, has sprouted various useful appendages in recent years including the forward mounted in-flight refuelling probe and wingtip flare/chaff dispenser pods.

Establishment at RAF Cottesmore received the first production aircraft. Since that time the Tornado has matured into the quite exceptional aeroplane schemed by its designers and sponsors, and in addition to large British, Italian and West German orders the type has secured useful export successes. The baseline model is the Tornado IDS interdictor and strike aeroplane, which the RAF designates the Tornado GR.1 which can also operate in the reconnaissance role with a British Aerospace multi-sensor reconnaissance pod. Weapon and sensor developments are now beginning to move well ahead of the levels predicted when the Tornado was designed and upgrading undertaken in the early 1990s allows the Tornado to carry the most advanced weapons such as the British Aerospace ALARM anti-radar missile, the British Sea Eagle anti-ship missile, a new generation of stand-off weapon dispensers, and also a number of European and American weapons as the situation demands. It has also been felt that the RAF's reconnaissance tasking is not best served by a podded sensor system, and some GR.1s have been converted, as the GR.1a, for the carriage of an internal reconnaissance system at the expense of the cannon armament.

The GR.1 and GR.1a will continue to serve RAF Strike Command very well in the interdiction role, but this is only half the Tornado story so far as the RAF is concerned. The other half is the dedicated Tornado ADV air-defence variant produced as the primary long-range interceptor of the UK Air Defence Region. By comparison with the IDS variant, the Tornado ADV has a number of important modifications to the airframe and electronics. The main change to the airframe is the lengthening of

Right: 15 Para embark on a C-130 for a flight from Scotland to a jump zone in the south of England. The flight was executed at a low altitude, which is a speciality of the Hercules. However, the aircraft would have gained height slightly over the actual jump area

Left: A Puma of No 33 squadron keeps its rotors moving as a section of troops embark to be taken to another part of the battle

Above: The crest of the Queen's Flight as shown on a Westland Wessex based at RAF Benson

Left: The latest addition to the Queen's Flight is the British Aerospace 146

Main picture: A Hawk T.1A from No 1 Tactical Weapons Unit based at RAF Brawdy approaches the RAF's bombing ranges in South Wales

the mid-fuselage section to allow the semi-recessed carriage of four British Aerospace Sky Flash semi-active radar homing air-to-air missiles. This lengthening has the useful by-products of increasing internal fuel capacity and therefore range, while slimming the fuselage lines to the extent that transonic drag is reduced and acceleration thereby improved. Electronic changes are centred on the replacement of the single inertial navigation system by twin units, an updated main computer, more advanced head-down displays and replacement of the Tornado IDS's Texas Instruments multi-role radar by the Foxhunter radar. This radar has the track-while-scan ability to plot between 12 and 20 targets at range in excess of 120 miles (195 km).

The Tornado ADV entered service as the Tornado F.2 with limited radar and the RB199 Mk 104 engine, such aircraft being redesignated Tornado

Inset: The Hawk T.1 is a training aircraft, but is able to undertake air defence missions in time of crisis. Because of its lack of radar, the Hawk must be talked onto its target by air combat controllers

Right: A fully armed Tornado F.3 ADV waits at RAF Lossiemouth for a scramble that might well see it launched to shadow a Soviet Tupolev Tu-95 Bear as it tests the RAF's northern flank

Opposite: Two views of ZE162: a Tornado F.3 from No 229 Operational Conversion Unit based at RAF Coningsby. The crossed sword and flaming torch on the tail is the symbol of this unit

F.2A on being upgraded to improved electronic standards. The current production model is the Tornado F.3 with the full electronic standard, automatic wing sweeping and flap/slat scheduling controlled by the central computer for enhanced manoeuvrability, and the digitally controlled RB199 Mk 104 engine. The current armament is a single 27-mm cannon plus four Sky Flash (or Sparrow) medium-range missiles and four AIM-9LM Sidewinder short-range missiles, though future upgrades include AIM-132 ASRAAM short-range missiles and, possibly, the Active Sky Flash active radar homing variant of the present medium-range weapon. The Tornado ADV also carries a data-link equipment for real-time interchange of information with ground stations and, more importantly, Boeing Sentry AEW.1 airborne early warning aircraft. This combines long-range surveillance capacity with an onboard tactical command crew and began to enter service in March 1991, with deliveries completed by early 1992. With the Tornado ADV's electronic teething problems a thing

Above:
First deployed during 1958, the long range Bloodhound surface-to-air missile was phased out in July 1991. A replacement for the Bloodhound is planned to enter service in the late 1990 s.

of the past, the combination of Sentry and Tornado ADV offers a long-range air-defence capability probably unmatched anywhere in the world.

The outer-zone air defence provided by the Sentry/Tornado ADV combination is complemented by British Aerospace Hawk T.1As providing an emergency capability in the inner zone. The T.1A variant of the Hawk is a simple development of the RAF's standard flying and weapons trainer with provision for two AIM-9 Sidewinder air-to-air missiles. The Hawk lacks radar, and the T.1A is therfore entirely dependent on directions from the Sentry AEW.1 or ground-based radars and their associated ground-controlled interception organisation for vectoring into the areas where a target can be acquired visually. But this inner-zone combat tasking is a sideline to the Hawk's primary role, which as noted above, is advanced flying and weapon training. The Hawk is typical of modern trainers in having a deep forward fuselage that permits the installation of well

Right: A Rapier missile is shown at the moment of launching. The British Aerospace Rapier is operated by the RAF Regiment for shorter range ground-to-air defence

staggered tandem seating that allows the instructor in the rear seat to see over the head of the pupil in the front seat, and is notable for its high performance combined with fighter-type handling that is nonetheless viceless. There can be no higher compliment to this very attractive little aeroplane than the affection in which it is held by its RAF crews and its considerable export success, including the T-45A Goshawk carrier-capable version being procured for the US Navy. At the same time, the handling and performance of the trainer have prompted development of single- and two-seat dedicated attack variants that are now beginning to secure export orders.

Such is the unique nature and capability of the British Aerospace Harrier that the only possible replacement for this obsolescent type is another Harrier. But the new Harrier is a considerably different beast from its predecessor reflecting mostly the demands made on McDonnell Douglas, British Aerospace's US licensee, by the US Marine Corps in its search for a successor to its baseline Harrier version, the AV-8A. With support from British Aerospace, McDonnell Douglas has produced a new version of the Harrier as the Harrier II, retaining an overall similarity to the original machine but with virtually every part of the design refined to boost lift or reduce weight. The most notable alteration is the wing, with a single-piece structure of graphite/epoxy composite construction with a deep supercritical section and, by comparison with the original Harrier wing, greater area and reduced sweep. The new wing provides better lift at all speeds, has more hardpoints, has more than 50 per cent greater internal fuel capacity and, through the adoption of leading-edge root extensions developed by British Aerospace, much improved rates of turn. The wing is also fitted with large slotted flaps that can be lowered to trap lift gas: combined with features such as improved underfuselage lift-improvement devices, zero-scarf nozzles and an uprated engine with better inlets, VTO lift is increased by no less than 6700 lb (3030 kg). Harrier II also possesses a more advanced cockpit and a number of other developments to boost overall capabilities very considerably over those of the Harrier. The type is in production for the US Marine Corps as the AV-8B, while British Aerospace has built the Harrier GR.5, an adapted version with more advanced British electronics and a cockpit modelled on that of the Sea Harrier naval counterpart to the original Harrier. These GR.5s have now been modified to Harrier GR.7 standard with night attack capability through the addition of a forward-looking infra-red sensor, pilot's night-vision goggles and other features, and further developments could result in a radar-carrying version.

Like all other British first-line warplanes now in service, the Harrier GR.7 has in-flight refuelling capability. The British were pioneers of such a system, and Flight Refuelling Ltd is still a world leader in the field of hose-and-drogue refuelling. In this system the receiver aeroplane is fitted with a probe that is inserted into a drogue at the end of the tanker's trailed hose to complete a mechanism that allows fuel to pass down the hose into the receiver's fuel tanks: breaking away from the drogue shuts of the fuel-flow valve and prevents any wastage of the precious fuel that may be required by other aircraft. For many years the RAF's main tanker was the Handley Page Victor in its K.2 version, but in 1982 the long-range operations associated with the Falklands war with Argentina accelerated a process that was already under way to create a large tanker force able to service the full range of RAF tactical aircraft and transports. Six Hercules C.1Ks were created by converting standard transports, and these aircraft are entrusted with support of the RAF's standard Lockheed Hercules transports. There are 60 such aircraft currently in service, 30 of the original 66 Hercules C.1s having been upgraded to Hercules C.3 standard with a longer fuselage for

Right: Photographed in the late 1980s, this Buccaneer from RAF Lossiemouth is armed with two British Sea Eagle missiles. The Sea Eagle is an over-the-horizon fire-and-forget missile that is designed to destroy even the largest surface warships. This role has now passed to the Tornado GR.1

Below right: A Sea King helicopter of No 202 Squadron hoists a sailor to the safety of the helicopter's hold. The SAR (Search and Rescue) helicopters are stationed in detachments around the British coasts

Opposite top: A Canberra from the now disbanded No 100 Squadron tows targets at RAF Akrotiri in Cyprus

Opposite bottom: A Wessex helicopter of No 84 Squadron operating in support of British forces in Cyprus

greater payload; Hercules aircraft with a refuelling probe have the suffix P to their designations. The same suffix is used for Nimrod MR.2 maritime patrollers retrofitted with a similar probe, and these aircraft have also been provided with greater offensive/defensive capability as a result of experience in the Falklands War: underwing hardpoints are now standard for the carriage of anti-ship missiles and/or

Above: Three BAe Hawk T.1s follow the coast from No 4 Flying Training School at RAF Valley

Right: An RAF British Aerospace Jetstream T.1 operated by No 6 Flying Training School. This is based at RAF Finningley

Sidewinder air-to-air missiles.

Greater in-flight tanking capability could not be provided by the Victor fleet. The aircraft were admittedly well suited to the role in terms of performance, but few aircraft were available for conversion, the aircraft were in any case beginning to run out of airframe hours, and the airframes were not ideally laid out for tanker conversion. Better capability is offered by airliners, and the RAF has in recent years added Lockheed TriStar and Vickers (now British Aerospace) VC10 tanker conversions to its fleet. In the case of the VC10s the main cabin was converted for fuel storage to feed the three-point refuelling system, but with the later TriStar a similar three-point refuelling system could be fed from fuel storage in the underfloor hold, leaving the main cabin for troop or freight transport.

Brief mention has been made of the campaign fought in 1982 to regain the Falkland Islands from Argentine occupation. Since that time the campaign has been eagerly dissected for tactical and technical lessons, and many of these have since been applied to RAF aircraft. The most notable impact has been

The Shorts Tucano is developed from the Brazilian Embraer trainer but only about 10 per cent of the original design remains. It has an 1100 shp Garrett engine which increases the airframe's speed at sea level from 210 to 270 knots. The cockpit has been redesigned to enable a trainee pilot to move smoothly from the Tucano to the BAe Hawk. There were many delays caused by RAF design requirements, and the Tucano began to enter into service only in the late 1980s

in the growth of in-flight refuelling as indicated above, but it should be noted that the campaign involved the RAF relatively little in direct terms as most of the air operations in the campaign were flown by Royal Navy aircraft. Admittedly, there were also the bombing raids against Stanley Airport by Avro Vulcans and the long-range maritime patrols of Nimrods, but the main RAF effort was devoted to tanking and, once the troops were ashore, close air support by Harrier aircraft operating from the carriers and then from forward shore bases. The RAF also provided a heavy-lift helicopter component, but this was very small as most of the relevant Boeing Vertol Chinook helicopters were lost with the Atlantic Conveyor to Argentine missile attack before reaching the shore.

The Chinook HC.1 is the most important helicopter currently in service with the RAF. The type was ordered as early as the 1960s, but on two occasions the order was postponed for economic reasons before the type finally began to reach service in December 1980. Since then the Chinook has proved invaluable, its twin-rotor design with a long fuselage providing the hold volume for a substantial number of men and/or weight of freight, while the power transmitted to the rotors by the twin turboshafts also makes possible the carriage of a large load suspended from the combination of three lifting points under the fuselage.

The most potent part of the RAF is Strike Command, primary British-based operator of the Tornado IDS, which in addition to the Tri-National Tornado Training Establishment at RAF Cottesmore and the Tornado Weapons Conversion Unit serves with Nos 27 and 617 Squadrons at RAF Lossiemouth. RAF tanker assets are the VC10s of No 101 Squadron at Brize Norton, also base for No 216 Squadron's TriStar tankers. The core of the Command's army support element is provided by two Harrier units, namely No 1 Squadron and Harrier Operational Conversion Unit at RAF Wittering: the first Harrier GR.5s were delivered in June 1988 and No 1 Squadron became fully operational on the variant during 1989. The group also controls the UK-based Jaguar force, whose operational elements are based at RAF Coltishall in the

Resplendent in its newly applied Desert Pink livery, this Buccaneer S2A is seen in its RAF Lossiemouth lair prior to its departure to the Gulf.

form of Nos 6 and 54 Squadrons in the attack role, and No 41 Squadron in the reconnaissance role; Jaguar conversion and continuation training is entrusted to No 16 Reserve Squadron at RAF Lossiemouth.

Group helicopter operations are centred on RAF Odiham, which is the home of No 7 Squadron with Chinooks and No 33 Squadrons with Pumas; No 72 Squadron operated Wessex helicopters in support of the army in Northern Ireland from RAF Aldergrove in the trouble province. Odiham is also the base for the helicopter training unit, No 240 Operational Conversion Unit with Chinooks and Pumas. Fixed-wing transport assets of the Command are based in south central England. No 101 Squadron flies VC10 long-range/VIP transport from RAF Brize Norton, supplemented by No 216 Squadron's TriStars, while RAF Lyneham accomodates the Hercules tactical support wing comprising Nos 24, 30, 47 and 70 Squadrons, together with the Hercules Operational Conversion Unit. Transport units include No 32 Squadron at RAF Northolt with a miscellany of British Aerospace HS 125 and Andover fixed-wing aircraft plus Aerospatiale Gazelle helicopter for VIP transport and communications. RAF Benson is home to the Queen's Flight.

Advanced training falls into Support Command's sphere of responsibility. The two primary units are Nos 4 and 7 Flying Training Schools based respectively at RAF Valley and Chivenor with the Hawk T.1As earmarked for a defensive task in the event of hostilities. Returning to Strike Command are the detachments in Belize and the Falklands. In Belize this comprises Nos 1417 and 1563 Flights, the former with Harriers and the latter with Pumas. In the Falklands is a more substantial force that has been put on a slightly higher state of alert following the election in May 1989 of a more hawkish Argentine president: based in the islands at RAF Mount Pleasant are No 78 Squadron with Chinook and Sea King helicopters, No 1312 Flight with Hercules C.1K tankers and No 1435 Flight (formerly part of No 23 Squadron) with Tornado F.3s.

Since the last Lightnings were retired at the end of 1988, and the Phantom in October 1992, the RAF's sole fighter is the Tornado F.3. Tornado fighter training is provided by No 229 Operational Conversion Unit at RAF Coningsby, and operational squadrons are Nos 5 and 29 Squadrons at Coningsby, and Nos 11, 23 and 25 Squadrons at RAF Leeming. The final two Tornado F.3 units are Nos 43 and 111 Squadrons at RAF Leuchars.

This air-defence force would be bolstered in war by the 'shadow' squadrons with their Hawk T.1As, and air control of the force would be provided by the Sentry AEW.1s of No 8 Squadron now based at RAF Waddington. Also falling under No 11 Group's aegis are the surface-to-air defences of the UK's main air bases. Rapid response protection of Leuchars and Lossiemouth is provided by the Rapier missiles of

Nos 27 and 48 Squadrons of the RAF Regiment. Waddington is unique among British bases in having AA artillery protection in the form of 35-mm Oerlikon-Buhrle GDF twin mounting and its associated Skyguard radar fire-control system: guns being captured in the Falklands are now operated by No 1339 Wing of the Royal Auxiliary Air Force.

Maritime operations are the purview of Strike Command. The group's main operational type is the Nimrod, of which there are three units in the form of Nos 120, 201 and 206 Squadrons based at RAF Kinloss. These maritime reconnaissance and anti-submarine aircraft are complemented by the Tornado anti-ship force based at Lossiemouth in the hands of Nos 27 and 617 Squadrons. Search and rescue is the responsibility of the Sea Kings and Wessexes of Nos 22 and 202 Squadrons, which operate as detached flights from bases round the coastline of the UK.

Other Strike Command assets are the Canberras based at RAF Wyton for photographic reconnaissance (No 1 Photographic Reconnaissance Unit) and electronic warfare training (No 360 Squadron). Also at Wyton are the three Nimrod R.1 electronic intelligence aircraft of No 51 Squadron. The command also controls some lesser units located overseas in Hong Kong (the Wessexes of No 28 Squadron) and Cyprus (the Wessexes of No 84 Squadron).

The RAF's other main operational formation is RAF Germany, whose combat assets are allocated to NATO's 2nd Allied Tactical Air Force. At RAF Laarbruch are two Harrier close support units in the form of Nos 3 and 4 Squadrons. The Tornado GR.1 is now the most important RAF Germany asset, however, and there are no fewer than four such squadrons in the form of Nos 9, 14, 17 and 31 Squadrons at RAF Bruggen. Other aircraft types

A Tornado GR1 simmers quietly in the heat at Dhahran, Saudi Arabia during the run-up to Operation Desert Storm.

operated in Germany are the Chinooks and Pumas of No 18 Squadron RAF Laarbruch. Only the short-range missile defence of west German bases is employed, and here the RAF Regiment uses the Rapier.

Support Command undertakes the rest of RAF's duties with a wide assortment of second-line and training aircraft. The command is responsible for university air squadrons operating the Bulldog and air experience flights operating the Chipmunk. In ascending order of flight performance, Support Command's training establishments are the Elementary Flying Training Schools at RAF Topcliffe with Chipmunk basic trainers, Nos 1 and 3 Flying Training Schools at RAF Linton-on-Ouse and Cranwell, and the RAF College Cranwell with Shorts Tucano turboprop trainers, and Nos 4 and 7 Flying Training Schools at RAF Valley and Chivenor with Hawk advanced trainers. The Shorts Tucano T.1 is a turboprop-powered type of Brazilian origin that offers adequate performance with considerable fuel-economy. Other training establishments are No 2 Flying Training School at RAF Shawbury with Aerospatiale Gazelle and Wessex rotary-wing train-

ers, No 6 Flying Training School at RAF Finningley with British Aerospace Jetstream T.1 and Dominie T.1 multi-engine and navigation trainers, and for instructor training the Central Flying School at RAF Scampton, which is also home to the Red Arrows aerobatic team.

Such then is the RAF today. Much of very real worth has been achieved in recent years, and indeed is still being achieved with the introduction of the Tornado in both its current variants. The 1990s will also see the introduction of the RAF's next important combat type, which is currently under development as the Eurofighter EFA. This is designed to replace the Jaguar and to complement the Tornado. Like that of the Tornado, the development is a collaborative venture again involving Italy, the UK and Germany but increased in this instance by Spain. The EFA is to be an extremely advanced type with a canard configuration, relaxed stability, fly-by-wire controls, largely composite construction and a host of other state-of-the-art features to see the RAF well into the 21st century.

War is hell, it can also have its informal aspects. Depicted here are two examples of strictly unofficial aircraft nose art; (left) this 'Snoopy Airways' cartoon adorned a Muharraq-based Tornado GR1, while (right) also operating from Muharraq was this 'girlie' liveried Jaguar GR1A.

This index consists of both a general index and also an index to aircraft.
Page numbers in italics refer to illustrations.

INDEX

GENERAL INDEX

INDEX TO AIRCRAFT

PHOTOGRAPHIC ACKNOWLEDGEMENTS

All photographs from BTPH Ltd with the exception of the following:

Nikk Burridge: Title page

Michael J. Hooks: 94–95, 102, 102–103, 105, 108–109, 111, 112–113, 114–115, 116–117, 118, 118–119, 120–121, 122, 122–123, 123, 124–125, 125, 126, 136, 136–137, 137, 140–141, 145, 146–147, 160–161, 170, 173, 176, 178 and 180–181.

TRH Pictures: DoD 4–5, RAF Museum 96 and 97, 98, MoD 100, RAF Museum 101 top, Vickers 101 bottom, BAe 104, RAF Museum 113, 128 and 129, RAF 130–131, 133, RAF 134 and 135, 135, BAe 138–139, 142, 142–143, 143, BAe 144 top, 144 bottom, BAe 149, BAe 152–153 and 154, Boeing 155, 156–157, M. Roberts 159 top, 159 bottom, 162–163, 166, 166–167, 167 top, M. Roberts 167 bottom, E. Neville 168, 168–169 and 172, 174, 174–175, Thorn EMI 175 top, RAF 175 bottom, 176, 177, 178.

ARNPRIOR PUBLIC LIBRARY
050431